Marianne E. Meyer

HOW WATER CONNECTS OUR WORLDS

Water Crystal Photos as a Mirror of the Soul

Free Energy: Water - Code cracked?

Adequate Aqua Activating Increases Efficiency, Quality of Life, and Vitality

Marianne Meyer, Apartado 320
P-8801 Tavira

© 2015 by Marianne E. Meyer, Tavira, Portugal
All rights are with the author

drmarianneemeyer @ gmail.com
www.marianne-e-meyer.com

Cover design, record & layout: M. Meyer
Photo credits:
Cover Back and page 2: Franz Nos
p. 7,12,20 Susanne Würtz
p. 91 f.: Wolfgang Czapp
S. 83: J.-P. Meyer
p. 85 ff.: Julius-Hensel-Blog
p. 48,50-58, 60, 62: Ernst F. Braun
p. 55: Ernst Schmerker

I thank Sterlin D. Allan for the report on page 86 f.

Production and Publishing:
BoD - Books on Demand, Norderstedt
ISBN 978-3-734736919

Some more books by M. E. Meyer:

Doris Day and My Search for Relatives
Migrant Birds on Wheels
Soon to be published:
Spirulina, Survival Food for a New Age
Self-help healing book
Cranberry Power Fruit
Fit and slim forever

M. Meyer has passed through many stages of life with the focus on self-help and learning: We are our own best teachers, healers, and spiritual leaders.

Formerly a Doctor's assistant, she later studied at *FHS* and *Johann-W.-Goethe University* in Frankfurt, laying emphasis on family therapy and gerontology, followed by a PhD study in gerontology and a study in nutrition, focusing on immune defense and Spirulina.

After earning her PhD in nutrition and living more than ten years in the US, the author went back to the Frankfurt/Heidelberg area and introduced Spirulina to her European and Russian readers. Ms. Meyer currently lives in Portugal and works at times with juveniles, who are displaying behavioral problems.

TABLE OF CONTENTS

Initial spark for the third book on water

The secret of our most important resource existing of two hydrogen atoms and one oxygen atom is still not revealed. This work shows an aspect of the chemical compound that brings the mystery of its versatility to light.

Furthermore, it holds the truth against the common, and status quo cementing falsities. Especially when the works of ingenious inventors, who could solve the energy problems of mankind are oppressed, destroyed or made ridiculous as esoteric garbage.

At least, one system of water activation and purification could have established. If we let run our tap water through this unit, we need no electricity, filters or maintenance and have water to drink and bathe of mountain spring water quality, anywhere in the house.

For about 15 years, I'm using the GIE-water device, for which Peter Gross in 2007 was awarded a gold medal at the International Exhibition of Inventions in Geneva. I noticed a difference in bathing immediately. The water feels like silk and holds the heat better. Since then, I no longer suffer from dry skin and my hair texture has improved. My brother uses a larger device in his *Pension Rosengarten* in Michelstadt, a friend in Spain an even larger one. He had chlorine and limescale in the tab water that smelled awful. Not even the dog liked it. After the water had passed through the device, it was palatable and the duty to descale the coffeemaker every three weeks was omitted.

With this background experience, I wanted to inform myself on the internet and googled: Aqua Lyros light-water. I came across the website of the former Swiss chemist who seems to lump together all tap water activators. Granted there may be some charlatans under the water tinkerers, but I would not describe the efforts of a genius inventor as decadent. Martin Koradi writes:

All the talk of energizing, vitalizing and animating water seems to me anyway quite decadent. We nevertheless have in Switzerland nationwide premium drinking water from the tap.

I was looking for an e-mail address to tell Mr Koradi of my good experience with the device by Peter Gross. And, when a 76-member jury award an instrument with the highest distinction, why should it not keep its promises? In addition, the phytotherapy docent ignores the fact that Switzerland uses pesticides that are forbidden in many other countries. The broadleaf herbicide glyphosate was also detected in the urine of the Swiss population. Incidentally, it was also Switzerland, as one of the first countries worldwide to introduce the fluoridation of tap water. In most countries, the experiments with this procedure were unsuccessful and aborted. Nevertheless, we should remain on the alert. Indeed, in recent years the overpopulation has hardly been discussed. Why? Is a solution already found and in action? We better make sure that nothing can harm us via forced medication from the faucet; there once was the recommendation for contraceptives. Whether or not it is forced medication, fact is: birth control pills and tranquilizers are among the drug cocktail that is regularly detected in tap water. Fluoride is a primary ingredient of many antidepressant drugs...

...namely because in certain circles it is now known that but surely neutralize the free will of man.

Fluoride inhibits vital enzymes such as the iodine-incorporation in the thyroid gland. Prof Dr. Werner Becker from *Bundesverband der naturheilkundlich tätigen Zahnärzte* in Deutschland (BNZ) says that the orthodontic treatments have skyrocketed since the use of fluoride. The leading activist against fluoridation, Dr. med. George Waldbott says, "depending on renal function 0.5-6.5% of the absorbed fluorides are stored in the body. Thus, infants, people with kidney disease and the elderly are at most at risk. "The biologist Dr. Ali H. Mohammed of the University of Missouri at Kansas City, USA, came through his experiments to the conclusion that sodium fluoride causes genetic damage in laboratory animals. Even the small amount of standard fluoridation of 1 mg of fluoride per liter of drinking water caused in mice prolonged chromosome breaks and injuries.

I could go on for pages with study results by experts to show Mr. Koradi that he can neither in Switzerland nor any other country be sure to get clean tap water. I do not know if economic and political interests have planned and forced the fluoride prophylaxis program. But I do know how to protect myself from toxins in tap water. I have, therefore, acquired the award-winning device for water transforming.

Metaphysical history

In California, in the late 80s early 90s, I was initiated in the Reiki energy. I was involved in Yoga, TM, Theosophy, Inner Light Healing and the development of psychic abilities. In a seance and a channeling, I asked the same question to the respective mediums. At the time, I considered to write a comprehensive book on various natural healing procedures and wanted to know: Would my first work make a difference? Both clairvoyants said the same sentence: I do not see a big book, but ten small books.

Eight years later, my metaphysical wedding was long past I published the first three books on Spirulina and strengthening the immune system. Only years later when I wrote my review, I remembered the words of the mediums: My ten books, I published so far, are no weighty tomes.

I would be glad if this book could help you in developing or enhancing a sense of oneness with everything. For our development and awareness, it is essential to confront us intuitively with the world of spirits. So far, this exchange took place via mediums, automatic writing and painting, telepathy, prophetic dreams, Reiki, clairvoyance, clairaudience, and psychometrics. As demonstrated in this work, we can also communicate via the neutral medium and energy transporter water. That I've come to realize when I was studying the water crystal photos obtained by neutral water informed with my signature. See chapter *Water Crystals: language of the soul* If we all had the awareness of what happens here, many people's lives would change for the better. What would this knowledge mean for science, art, and religion? What would it do with power structures? Would it also provide for transparency in other areas?

Anyhow, I will introduce you to the work of souls by showing their enlightening water images. After all, a picture says more than thousand words. But even with the eye, we all perceive things differently. That's why Paul Watzlawick asks: How real is real? Is the reality only caused by the subjective point of view and is, therefore, not to be understood as objective? My Professor, Ernest Jouhy, of Frankfurt University spoke of the double refraction of consciousness. That the environment does not exist without our consciousness, we also recognize by the different interpretation of the soul stars. Our mind creates the reality in which we live.

If we raise our awareness of our perception, the science has to recognize that the monopoly of the often cited objectivity rests on a shaky foundation. Christian Morgenstern puts it this way: There are no mysteries in themselves, only uninitiated of all grades. So what speaks against an initiation through our experience?

Water is everywhere. We know it as a means for cleaning and to satisfy our thirst. But the overall element also offers knowledge and provides our body with vital information. That the water as a medium connects the spiritual and material world is virtually unknown. Therefore, I show you how H_2O can be used to discover the truth.

Humanity has reached a point where it will be necessary for survival to discover the truth in all areas of life. That is noticeable in the water, Masaru Emoto, PhD, has shown with his epochal water crystal photography in *The Hidden Messages in Water*. I also was allowed to publish his photographs of frozen water drops in my book *Wunderwesen Wasser*.

The present work deals among other things with the *soul stars*, that Ernst F. Braun *fetched me from heaven*. His art to photographing water crystals is based on Emoto's method. He gave me the opportunity to use my power as a water being. As in a crystal ball I could read in my soul stars and identify who informed the water: our dead. The crystal images represent clearly milestones of my life, and the experiments with the *dead* attest to this doubt free.

I would be happy if I excite you to decode your very own water crystal photos:

www.wasserchristall.ch

For if we know that on the other side we can continue to be involved in the lives of our loved ones, our life in this world will have a significant impact.

I am particularly pleased that my former gospel choir-mate Dr. Renate Kaiser Alexnat also, at least part time, research via water crystal photos. I thank her and Ernst Braun that I may publish her soul stars. Renate specializes in dye plants. She worked scientifically for a year in Japan. A few years ago, she showed me three of her water crystal photos with the request for interpretation. That the mushroom cloud on one of the crystal images bodes no good, I was at once sure about. What my friend could have to do with the Fukushima nuclear disaster, I learned recently. She describes it from page 59 on.

In this third book of water, I will direct the interest of my readers to the latest discoveries that affect our most essential food. Most important is the technology that transforms dead water, pressed through miles of pipes, again in a vivid, structured H_2O. It also protects us from the forced medication from the tap.

Pure water is as important as an environmentally friendly energy. The change could have happened long ago because the space energy produced by vacuum field energy machines has been around a long time. However, stakeholders call a halt to environmentally friendly, inexhaustible and free energy. Unloving, inconsiderate and unwise they perpetuate the status quo of the global distribution of power. The trouble is: On the energy that is inexorably destroying our nurturer planet, an enormous amount of cash is earned. Oil and gas companies and the state collect billions. They make every effort to suppress free energy by commenting cynical about it or ridiculing it. Our representatives swear to avert damage from the people. But they seem to ride out tedious tasks and carefree lulling us to destruction.

Actually, Professor Dr. Claus W. Turtur had offered me to write a foreword pertaining the last chapter. That is how it came: I asked my fellow author, the engineer Wolfgang Meyer, if he believed that Nikola Tesla had truly driven the space-energy converter in his Pierce Arrow. On the internet, one gets mixed messages; some evidence for the truth and some who call it conspiracy theory. But we lately were deceived especially by the USA facilities. Therefore, I assume that we would have the Tesla car and a less polluted environment in so long. Unfortunately, it was prevented by the power monopoly of the United States. I also read recently that the term conspiracy theory is a US Invention, to choke off every awkward question and to ridicule every unwanted topic. Inventors, politicians or scientists, who deal with undesired issues, are risking much. Often they loose their reputation and their job, sometimes even their lives. Therefore, the number of those who go out on a limb, especially before retirement, is very low.

My namesake colleague referred me to this research scientist. Amiably, Professor Claus Turtur told me that he considers Nikola Tesla's space-energy converter for reputable since the son of a witness reported to him thereof. Dr. Turtur had visited Klaus Jebens in Hamburg, who is himself an inventor with many patents and today about 87 years old. His father was director of the *Deutsches Erfinderhaus e. V.* in Hamburg. In this function, he visited Thomas A. Edison in America. Heinrich Jebens had also met Nikola Tesla. The father of the free energy gave Heinrich Jeben a ride in his space-energy car. Klaus Jebens wrote a book on various point-energy converter. In *Die Urkraft aus dem Universum*, he referred to his father's incident with the most ingenious inventor of the History of Science.

Although Mr. Turtur is convinced of the effectiveness of the space energy converter, he thinks, 99% of the space-energy videos on the Internet are fakes. They are supposed only to confuse the mind, to distract the people, and to discredit serious scientists.

www.borderlands.de/Links/TeslaCarReport.pdf

The work of Professor Turtur is considered to be brilliant and the presentation of the results excellent. Academic colleagues express themselves strangely irrelevant. They cynically talk of circus and carnival, but remain guarded over it. Apparently physicists are afraid to verbalize their views on new topics. When asked about it or called in for advice, they express skepticism. That also applied to Max Planck for his helping to develop quantum theory, and it still holds true today for the area of free energy research. Let's hope that many citizens are dedicated to the subject so that the professionals can no longer ignore, reject, or ridicule it.

Max Planck has often described the rude skepticism of experts aptly: *A new scientific truth does not triumph by convincing its opponents and making them see the light, but rather because its opponents eventually die, and a new generation grows up that is familiar with it.*

Had the human race time, the mental inertia of physicists would be acceptable. We could wait until the Planck criterion of acceptance is reached. But humanity has no time since the up to now used forms of energy destroy our habitat in murderous pace. If the experts refuse to overcome their lethargy, it could be critical to our survival on earth, warns Professor Turtur and further notes: *Scientists are reputed to be knowledgeable. In order not to jeopardize their reputation, they deal with things that they know and avoid things that they don't know. Therefore, science is restricted to known facts and does not deal with the unknown new. Thus, unfortunately, extremely aggravates the exploration of a new specialty as the space energy.* (2013)

The same applies to the experiments by means of informed water. It may be new to many that souls make use of the water medium to communicate with us. That is in the truest sense of the word the essential reason the element of water is so unpredictable.

Intuitively, I was able to understand the message of the spiritual water painters, photographed by Ernst E. Braun. Many of the water crystals from neutral water, informed by my signature, are clearly recognizable by others. For I have four gifted artist painters on the other side. It should be interesting to proof, if the same is true for other people with loved ones or friends on the other side who were artist painters during their fleshly life. If one or the other of my readers would want to have their soul stars photographed by Ernst F. Braun (www.wasserkristall.ch) and share his or her experiment, I'd be glad if you let me know.

Introduction

First they ignore you, then laugh at you, then they fight you, then you win.

Mahatma Gandhi

We humans, known as custodians of the earthly creative power, have become the biggest threat to the blue planet. Carelessly we plunder the earth and think only of our present advantage. Next to the air, water is our most important vital necessity. It needs oil, gas, coal and mineral ores in order to mature. As "mature" is referred to water when it is enriched with all the minerals and trace elements. That occurs when the groundwater rises upwards to the surface. It takes the minerals and electrolytes as a kind of life experience to mature. The juvenile, youthful water is unsuitable for drinking. It deprives the body of everything it needs to have itself.

Another danger threatens through fracking. For shale gas production, chemicals are needed. These can contaminate the groundwater. A mix of water, chemicals and quartz sand is pressed under high pressure into deep layers of rock. That creates small cracks (Engl. fractures), which releases the gas. German mineral water companies and brewers demand, not to approve hydro fracking. For, even if only a small amount of the chemicals get in a mineral deposits that spring would no longer be usable.

Another threat to the health is the defeat of the creative process through genetically changing our food. Inevitable losses during preservation, development and adulteration of varieties are to be expected. With pesticides, herbicides, plastics, heavy metals, radioactive particles and other pollutants we contaminate the air, soil and water. Then we wonder when the uproar of the elements cause violent storms and flooding of straightened rivers and the earth shakes or spits fire.

It's high time that we take advantage of the free energy systems, such as the zero point or vacuum energy of Professor Dr. Claus Turtur and with magnetic motors, the air pressure or water powered cars. A variety of such environmentally friendly processes waiting to serve the people. Some of them I present in Part V some you'll find on the following website.

http://freeenergynews.com

But the power of the energy companies is still so vast that they have always managed to buy the inventions or steal them and make them disappear in a drawer somewhere. However, *in connection of enabling the vacuum-energy research*, Prof. Turtur urges, *namely the provision of the necessary research resources, I can hardly estimate how much time we have left. The fact is that the problem of nuclear fission is becoming increasingly difficult, and the environmental damage caused by the recent traditional forms of energy so massive advances that you really have to wonder how long the Planet holds us out - with all the nonsense that people doing here.*

It is regarded as imperative to fight back against this destructive power, preferably via our consumer behavior. Young people are already questioning the car as a status symbol. In my book *Wunderwesen Wasser* I have already reported about intuitive researchers such as Nikola Tesla, Viktor Schauberger, Wilhelm Reich, Johann Tikale others, which contributed to the preservation of the earth and its creatures. But the envious and greedy power mongers could suppress their inventions through manipulation, accusations, blackmail or coercion. They discredited them and exploited their creative works or robbed it. The thought of a quick profit displaces the concern for the future of their children. This lack of love they bequeath further. The kid's children then acidify the blood of the earth"

by robbing it of the important raw materials again. Because of the sins of the fathers very little alkaline H_2O gushes out of the world's wells. And since most waters only have a pH below 6.5, we also suffer from increasing acidosis of the blood. That forms the foundation for disorders and diseases. Acidity makes us tired and weakens our drive and our immune system.

If we take a careful course for our planet, we also conserve the soul of all living things! Without water, there is no life! In this book, I will show you the fascination of the frictional and most mysterious element, so you can see your power as a water being! The power of the souls through text, sound, word, and deed reflected in the water, we can see through the water crystal photography. Masaru Emoto demonstrates this impressively. It is now more than ever necessary to take advantage of the influence of water souls to transform the barren time in which we live, in heaven on earth. In this regard, I thank all beings for their help, in which dimensions of the universe they may commute.

Dr. Klaus Volkamer regards the universe as "an ethereal creature, in higher dimensions than light speed with each other inter-connected and communicating with much gross material and thus isolated appearing individual structures. Ultimately, everything arises from the invisible, animate and universally entangled Ethereal, a universal life force." (2013)

The self-resonance of each individual is the total of all that he or she has experienced in the course of eons. The cells serve as a memory storage:

Memories arise when experience of intense emotions, such as pride, shame, fear or powerlessness are accompanied. I can remember very early haunting feelings. Once, my mother took away the pacifier and deposited it on the top compartment of our kitchen cabinet. When I was alone, I crawled onto the shelf where the upper part sits on, stretched for the key, pulled me up, unlocked and happily grabbed my pacifier lying between medication boxes. Such jubilation mood has a positive effect on the energy fields of the body. That may lead to an attitude that we can achieve anything in life. In contrast, adverse experiences influence our individual vibration frequency negatively, and we react out of tune. Negative thoughts, pollutants in the air, unhealthy diet and metabolic slags also poison our cells. Deposits of heavy food or emotional ballast in the form of fear, hatred and grief produce blockages in the energy fields and eventually lead to disease.

Part IV. WATER AND HEALTH informs about how we can adapt the distorted innate resonance of damaged cells to their ideal natural frequency. So we better pay attention to our thoughts, feelings, and words that express imperfection. Thereby we can set off disharmonious vibrations.

I. IS OUR TAP WATER STILL LIFE-SUPPORTING?

I have repeatedly stressed that it does not matter from what source you draw the water as long as it is pure and as long as the water quenches the thirst of the people.

Krishnamurti

Does the natural cycle clean the water?

When rain clouds discharge their cargo over wet meadows, fields and forests, trickles away into the ground water and wells up again, we are supplied forcibly with burdening harmful pollutant information.

Originally, H_2O was natural and had the power to cleanse itself. Today, you cannot expect that. Though, the infiltrating rainwater, the later part of the groundwater, filters through the soil, but:

How with all the pesticides, herbicides, heavy metals, pollution, radioactive particles and other impurities in the air, soil and waters should still a cleaning take place?

Emoto shows with examples of rivers that polluted and contaminated water is disturbed in its inner rhythm, and the crystalline structure is lost. In the upper reaches of the rivers, natural purification occurs, and beautiful crystals emerge. In contrast, the water in the middle part of the rivers is dirty from factories. The water crystals look like cancerous growths. Further down the river, the water is often back to its crystalline form. The aquatic biologist Theodor Schwenk also showed that due to initiate sewage and pollutants fresh spring water loses its life force. It only provides diffuse, almost formless flow patterns and appears as dead.

Charles Vörösmarty and Peter McIntyre studied the global threat of water security. Researchers at the City University of New

York found that 80% of the world's population is exposed to a high amount of threat. Few rivers in uninhabited tropical regions of the Amazon Basin and Northern Australia or the northern globe, in Siberia, Canada and Alaska are still untouched. People in poor countries are particularly vulnerable, since hardly any money is put into the improvement of water quality. But also in the industrialized countries is little acted on the real causes of the pollution. Therefore, Vörösmarty and colleagues recommend, especially to protect the floodplains. They can make expensive water treatment technology unnecessary and prevent flooding (*ZEIT ONLINE* 09/30/10).

Worldwide, only a few waters with neutral pH are gushing from the wells. That suggests they are not adequately cleaned naturally by distillation of rainwater. Pesticides, carcinogenic micro plastic from cosmetics and food, even milk and honey, highly toxic uranium and other heavy metals in the soil as well as drugs from the sewage acidifying our groundwater. Thus, we get no safe drinking water, since antibiotics & Co. are hardly eliminated via chemical reprocessing in sewage treatment plants. The following chapter informs about medicines that should make the sick healthy but make the healthy ill. Is that not sick?

* Today, even the groundwater is polluted.

* Toxic chemicals, plastic pellets and radioactive contaminate our waters.

* H_2O is insufficiently purified by distillation of rainwater.

How to avoid forced medication from the tap?

In Germany, every year 38,000 tons of drugs are prescribed. Seven out of ten Americans take at least one prescription drug. 17% of Americans take antibiotics, 13% antidepressants and also 13% opioids. Much of them come in the urine over the wastewater in sewage treatment plants and from there into the groundwater.

From hospitals, a lot of antibiotics and carcinogenic cytostatics (cell-killing agent) reach the wastewater and rivers. These and other

dangerous drugs get via toilet flushing directly to the sewer system. Most active pharmaceuticals are excreted with the urine.

The environmental physician, Klaus Kümmerer and Ali Al Ahmed of the University Hospital of Freiburg showed that three common cytotoxic drugs (cyclophosphamide, ifosfamide and epirubicin hydrochloride) could not be eliminated by the treatment plant. These drugs are taken by cancer patients during chemotherapy. But they are themselves considered carcinogenic!

How far-reaching the medication from the tap is, found the Odenwald graduate engineer Thomas Junker. Using a model sewage treatment plant, he examined a radio-labeled antibiotic substance in the laboratory for biodegradability. The researcher from Erbach demonstrated: Almost 93% of the drug he could account for again. The vast majority of the antibiotic would, therefore, pass into the rivers! In the further course of the test, only a quarter of the test substance was biodegraded by micro-organisms. Thus, we must expect a solid forced medication from the tap. Thomas Junker has made a contribution to environmental protection with his award-winning work. It points out how we better dispose of medicines. Still more reasonable would be to refrain largely from chemical drugs (2002).

The wrong disposal of drugs may be one of the reasons for the dramatic increase in cancer rates. In the pharmacy, you may be advised to throw the remains in the garbage or to solve the pills and better wash them away in the toilet. They may tell you, that way in the trash burrowing children cannot be poisoned by the colorful beads. But then the little ones are again the stupids because their blood-brain barrier is not yet developed. They are the most in danger from the heavily loaded tap water. Also, the researchers from Freiburg in a further test with the antibiotic Ciprofloxacin found that sewage treatment plants pose no barrier for such active pharmaceutical ingredients. That can indicate:

With our main matter, we regularly take up antibiotics, breed resistant strains of various pathogens in the body and if we get ill we may no more find an effective remedy.

The rapid increase in cancer rates and long-forgotten diseases demonstrate how dangerous the continuous intake of these drugs is. Slaughter animals are fed antibiotics to make them grow faster. It is quite natural that that destroys the immune system of animals. They bear no healthy offspring. And as a source of food these animals do more harm than good.

Whether it comes to cancer drugs, antibiotics, psychotropic drugs, x-ray contrast agents or other water polluting pharmaceuticals, data on the impact of drugs in the aquatic environment are scarce. In addition, estrogen, cholesterol-lowering drugs, and antibiotics are not covered with the methods of investigation; consequently, there are no special filters. Another complicating factor is: Those not degradable in wastewater vagrant materials can react with each other and produce new dangerous compounds!

What can we do with the forced medication from the tap? It is high time we stop to poison us. Natural supplements, that strengthen the immune system and make chemical drugs largely unnecessary can help us. Blue-green micro algae discharge demonstrably accumulated toxins from the body. Many dentists use Spirulina for discharging amalgam. Some doctors recommend their cancer patients to take the beneficial microorganism to counteract the negative chemotherapy side effects (Meyer 2002, 2006 and 2014).

A few years ago, the medical school smirked on the now established cancer treatment with mistletoe. In contrast to chemotherapy, natural means strengthen the body's defense and do not destroy any healthy cells. Another way, to ensure clean water is writing to our elected representatives and urge measures to prevent the forced medication from the tap. People who no longer see their salvation in politics, can set up a citizens' initiative or start a petition.

For if we spend our good money for more cell killing drugs, it may happen that we finance our suffering ourselves and take part in something that could develop into the greatest mass extinction of all time!

In addition, the generous prescription of female sex hormones may have an adverse effect on reproduction in humans. Since, due to the overflowing waters with estrogen in many rivers already exist predominantly female fish.

It is high time that we pull the emergency brake! We are in the greatest danger. Most people guess it, but the fear paralyzes them to do something about it. Do we really have to be frightened? Are we so powerless, as many believe? We better recognize the power of our thoughts and make use of it! We can change ourselves and our environment at any moment! By changing our consciousness and finally take action as citizens and consumers! We seek to better live in harmony with our Mother Earth and all its inhabitants. We are all one, material, immaterial, mentally, spiritually, physically and biochemically. The earth has to the smallest trace element the same composition as the man and the sea.

Everything we are doing to the earth, water, animals or another human being, we do to ourselves!

We cannot turn the clock back! But there are numerous sustainable projects that serve the protection of life. With nationwide growth of protein-rich Spirulina and the transition to free and renewable energy (solar, the wind, water, and biomass), hunger and unemployment could be eliminated worldwide. The sun provides several thousand times more energy than we need. The fear of overpopulation, nuclear disasters and the contamination of our drinking water by pesticides, waste oil, and chemical wastes should not keep us from action. Not even the fear of diseases resulting from poisons in the water. If your physician recommends chemotherapy, radiation or other measures that significantly interfere with the natural course of the organism, we better ask: To honor and conscience, would you recommend that for your mother?

In a telephone call, the Chemnitz Dr. Bernd Winter of the Society for Biological Cancer Defense informed me that the success rate of chemotherapy is a total of only 5 to 7%. Since this therapy was developed against tumors of the reproductive organs, where the success rate is 25-30%, there is no need to burden a sick body with such poisons. Even with breast cancer, we have a better survival rate with Spirulina. The blue-green alga is known as a powerful plant antioxidant with unique anti-cancer properties. Therefore,

Allal Ouhtit and his fellow researchers from the Sultan Qaboos University in Oman, investigated the effect of Spirulina against chemically induced breast cancer in rats. End of Nov. 2013, they reported their findings:

Spirulina reduced the number of new cases from 87% to 13%! Chemical drugs cannot keep up with this result in any way. In chemotherapy, the whole organism is bombarded with highly toxic cell-killing medicine. Thus, the tumors are supposed to die. But primarily healthy cells die. Often skin and hair are etched away. We also eliminate, as mentioned, most of the ingested antimicrobial agents with the urine. Due to inadequate water treatment, they get into our drinking water.

The moral commandments of medical practice formulated by Hippocrates are in conflict with the material interests of physicians and pharmacists. Therefore, we have to deal with the fact that damaging drugs in massive quantities get into our drinking water. The pharmaceutical industry attracts doctors with prescription premiums. Often we are also to blame if we require fast-acting medication instead of a natural cure in bed.

Hippocrates called for the strengthening of the immune system through herbs and other natural remedies, to mobilize the inner healer. But impatient patients accept a dulling and weakening of their body's defense. Because of fear of their workplace, they go for the chemical bombs instead for water cures and other gentle healing methods to detoxify and regenerate. We better realize that we hurt ourselves when we ingest chemicals and bring them in our water cycle!

We better trust the infallible nature as the world champion in healing and eliminate our mistakes!

Let us better not prescribe any medication, of which we know in advance that we do not take them because of the many unsolicited side effects. Thereby, we force up health insurance costs and contaminate our environment and our water because there is no safe disposal of chemical substances.

If you want to find out for yourself whether the used tap, spring or well water contains harmful substances, you can order a test kit for about €30. See also page 27.

www.selfcontrolshop.com/produkte/wasser
/trinkwasser-test-kit

We can get eight results, such as data on bacteria, lead, the two pesticides Atrazine and Simazine, the total content of nitrite/ nitrate, total chlorine content, pH count and the total water hardness. The results can be easily compared with the reference values.
In USA, you can look at test kits here:

http://www.lamotte.com/en/drinking-
water/individual-test-kits

* Thousands of tons of cancer-causing drugs do enter into our rivers.

* Due to the flood of waters with estrogens, in many rivers are predominantly female fish.

* Daily doses of antibiotics in the feed of cattle destroy the immune system of animals and lead to long-forgotten diseases.

* If we heal ourselves with the detoxifying algae Spirulina, we protect our drinking water.

* Chemotherapy was developed against tumors of the reproductive organs. It is successful in other cancers only 5 to 7%. The question remains open, what is done to the body with the chemical poisons and how it is related to the rate of recidivism.

* Let us care for better conditions, establish citizens' initiatives and start petitions. Let's talk with our community representatives about safe hazardous waste disposal and clean H2O.

* We better test our water with a test kit ourselves or we invest in a good activation system, especially when samples have critical values.

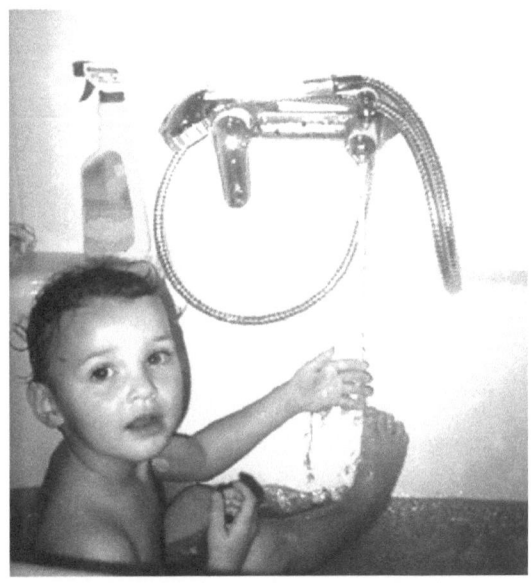

The nuclear contamination of our drinking water

Almost everything that the people is officially communicated about nuclear energy, is simply not true. It is not true that at this energy is "No way around". It is not true that it is cheap, clean, environmentally friendly and virtually without risk.

Prof Dr. E. Huster, nuclear physicist

On 02-28-77, the then director of the Institute of Nuclear Physics, University of Münster, with about 20 colleagues directed an open letter at the then Federal President Walter Scheel. Alas, politicians usually don't listen to the experts. Since Fukushima, an increasing number of people think that it would have been better not to split the atomic nucleus. The effluents of nuclear power plants pollute more and more our rivers and

II. ACTIVATED TAB OR BOTTLED WATER?

Happiness and health, as well as unlimited amounts of energy, are accessible to us at almost no cost, once we realize that water, the blood of the Earth, contains the will and it's resistance, life itself, for which we fight so hard today because we constantly take this carrier of all life continuously by our actions its noblest element: its soul.

Victor Schauberger

Adequate Aqua activation

Free clean water is a fundamental right of all people. Therefore, a responsible use of precious H_2O resources is essential. In this context, it is crucial to reaching as many people as possible with the subject of water.

Johann Grander, Viktor Schauberger, Wilhelm Reich, Louis Claude Vincent, Johann Tikale among others I have already presented in my first book on water. These pioneers of water research knew that the water has a memory and can store in its molecular structure all the information it gets from contact with other substances.

Wilfried Hacheney is the inventor of the so-called water-levitation. He made it his business to develop a form of true human science. In 1984, conventional water whirled at high speed through the spirally arranged hoses of his levitation machine. He then established with his daughter Dorte Hacheney the first watering place for swirling water. Today we find in Germany more than a hundred such water places that have made it their goal to provide information on the water culture and water quality.

Even mechanically, purified water contains pollutant frequencies of uranium and other heavy metals and drugs. The world-renowned physicist Dr. Wolfgang Ludwig found that the information of the pollutants or their electromagnetic oscillations is still detectable in the purified, even in distilled water. After today's conventional drinking water treatment, a lengthy follow-up with a flow and seeping stretch would be required. This way, the water can via turbulence and vibrations free itself from the stored information and the pollutants.

The point is now to animate the water anew, so it is again a true carrier of life. It is to give it back its natural self-cleaning capacities and life-enhancing information. Modern systems revive the tap water and put it in the physical condition of artesian water dripped through soil layers. With such an activated water, the metabolism of our cells works at the highest level. We feel balanced, fit and full of life. The Aqua-Lyros system confirms Dr. Ludwig's statement that water can store the once imprinted information on the level of certain frequencies and transmit them to other systems such as living organisms.

Rolf Keppler sent me his informative monthly newsletter just before the release of this book (www.rolf-keppler.de). The descendent of the famous astronomer and astrologer, Johannes K., made me aware of Ayhan Doyuk's super-ionized water. The Turkish inventor claims to have devised something to purify water completely after oil disasters. The videos, that show how the AyDo™ water works, you find on the following links.

http://tinyurl.com/l7l88u7
http://tinyurl.com/yle624t

The price list on the website www.aydo-deutschland.de did not contain a device that can super-ionize my tap water. A one-time purchase of €2,000 I could afford. But to buy 5-liter bottles for € 57.50 is for me currently out of reach. If Ayhan Doyu wants to regenerate all waters on earth and the body

water of its inhabitants, he better offers an affordable product for everybody.

Of the water activators and purification systems tested in *Wunderwesen Wasser*, I remained true to the one developed by Peter Gross. Currently, we use it in a cistern. My experience still refers to the first generation of devices for vitalization of water. By the way, Wilfried Hacheney who tested many devices should have bought the devices from Peter Gross for himself and his family. Even more power and oxygen provide the Aqua-Lyros models based on the GIE unit of Peter Gross. This second-generation activator developed by Peter and Isabel Gross is a nature adapted method for safely treating tap water. It works without filter and maintenance. Since thereby are no incidental expenses, it can serve as a convenient system for water activation for a lifetime. It would be desirable if baths were equipped with Aqua-Lyros activators. If the chlorine flows through this device in water treatment plants, it will not be detected

chemically, yet to taste or smell. Also, it would not irritate the mucous membranes.

Globally, each year about 40 million tons of chlorine, one of the most widely used chemicals, is used. Via sewage, it gets into the drinking water and forms there dangerous, enormously teratogenic and cancer-causing compounds. In Germany, drinking water is usually disinfected with ozone and rarely as in the southern European countries with chlorine. However, it is in the water. Why? For a few cents per liter, it is available as a whitener, decolorizing solution and detergent and then gets into the waste and groundwater. It is neither affected by biological processes nor degraded in sewage treatment plants or the aquatic environment. If we let chlorine smelling water run through the Aqua-Lyros unit, there is no more smell or taste of chlorine. We don't have to believe it, we can test the device for up to two weeks. How does this miracle of physics and metaphysics function?

The active principles of the Aqua-Lyros technology

The functional principle of the Aqua-Lyros system is based on decades of studies of nature. It also integrates already known methods of water research.

1. Breakdown of the watercourse after the input to 2 or 4 strands of wire depending on the model size (System Aqua Lyros)

2. Turbulence by rotation of water in spiral form (System Viktor Schauberger)

3. Turbulence through magnetic north polarity orientation of water molecules (System Dr. Patrick Flanagan)

4. Ionization of water by means of permanent magnets (system Peter Gross)

5. Permanent-magnetic caused alteration of the water's lime-structure= softer water, ideal for humans, animals, and plants

6. Turbulence by time varying alternating pressure zones (system Peter Gross)

7. Alternating pressure zones in a millisecond cycle for conditional (as flow-dependent) purely physical bacteria killing (system Peter Gross)

8. Vortex formation by different electromagnetic field line vectors inside and outside water-bearing pipes due to the flow of water with free ions without the use of electricity and outside the water-carrying pipes (system Peter Gross)

9. Vortex formation caused by magnetically south polarity orientation of water molecules (system Dr. Patrick Flanagan)

10. Transmission of information of more than 9,995 material natural frequencies.

11. Transmission of information from numerous intangible natural frequencies, such as afterglow, full lunch and full moon light, the frequency of the pulsation of the earth (Schuman 8.23 Hertz waves with a harmonic of 9.05 Hz), planetary frequencies, white noise, and other natural frequencies, also from plants.

12. High-grade shielding against the effects of electron-smog (system Peter Gross)

13. Oxygenation of the water (on average about 7%) without direct addition of oxygen. As a result of all the different chemical composition of the water, sometimes even within the same city, the average value may exceed or fall below (system Peter Gross)

14. Multiple Orgone charging by layer design (system Wilhelm Reich)

15. Additional intensive energizing of the flowing water by using only axes-aligned building material (system Peter Gross)

16. Consistent compliance with the laws of sacred geometry (e. g., the golden ratio and all systems based on it. See the Cheops pyramid and others (System Christian Lange)

17. Transmission of natural frequencies of silver and of many other minerals and trace elements (System Aqua Lyros)

18. Under this point, four modes of operation are united that make the replica of the Aqua-Lyros almost impossible. Trade secret Aqua Lyros GmbH (source www.aqua-lyros.de)

The Aqua-Lyros system implements only physical principles, similar to the natural cycle of water. The cylindrical device can be installed in an apartment in a bath or shower. Homeowners can attach it into the building wiring and so draw the lively water from all taps. The maintenance-free device shall be supplied with no additional energy.

This newly structured water detoxifies naturally and constantly attracts world-wide new enthusiastic users. They declare that Aqua Lyros water is softer, reduces calcium deposits and prevents neoplasms. They need less detergent and conditioner. It tastes better than tap water, arouses thirst for more, increase the capacity and strengthen the immune system. In *Wunderwesen Wasser,* I publish some reports from users who could cure diseases with the activated water.

According to researchers, the Aqua-Lyros is bearing the entire rainbow spectrum of light. This phenomenon is known so far only from the healing springs of Mary's apparition sites such as Fatima in Portugal, Lourdes in France, Montichiari in Italy and Medjugorje in Bosnia-Herzegovina as shown on page 30.

Wolfgang Ludwig tested the frequencies and information existing on the oscillation level from various curative waters. In the water samples from the wells of Lourdes, Fatima, Neuf-Chatel, Madonna degli Angeli and San Damiano he found specific, natural frequencies. These correspond with our brain waves, as can be detected in the electroencephalogram (EEG). The brain waves again correspond with the natural frequencies of the magnetic field of the earth. That could explain the healing power of light waters that we wonder at for so long. Meanwhile, many scientists, physicians, healers and a growing number of ordinary people around the world are amazed about the problems associated with the Aqua Lyros-water phenomena.

Positive effects of water revitalization

The essential reproducible effects, documented by scientific studies, laboratory tests, and practical experiences:

1. The natural oxygen content is 8-10% higher than the usual of 5-6%.

2. If we drink 2 liters a day, after two months, we can expect an increase of 20% oxygen in the blood, increased production of red blood cells, thinner blood and more vitality.

3. The volatility of oxygen is less than the oxygen-enriched waters for special athletes.

4. The health of the Aqua-Lyros user is robust, they hardly have colds or influenza-like illness, and then only for one or two days, instead of one or two weeks.

5. The unit harmonizes the energy systems of the body. The aura photography can demonstrate that.

6. Aqua Lyros water (ALW) increases the photon energy in the cells of living beings.

7. ALW has an exclusive light (nano) value of from 625 to 780 nanometers, as compared to typically 450 nanometers.

8. The germination of seeds is improved.

9. Aqua-Lyros eliminates uranium.

10. Tap water is enriched with life-support information. These frequencies or vibrations stimulate plant growth, performance and resilience of farm animals. They promote after-ripening of greenhouse products and a stable growth of young animals.

11. Aqua Lyros changes the molecular structure of lime in the water. It creates few deposits, and the existing build up in the pipes degrade. In the beginning, the pipes clean themselves. The water hardness is reduced by about 5 degrees.

12. Chlorine odor and taste are eliminated, as well the irritation of the mucous membranes. Chemically, chlorine is no longer detectable.

13. The cooking time of drinking water is shorter and the heat lasts longer.

14. AL-tap water is alkaline and ionized.

15. Aqua Lyros enhances the taste of vegetables, fruits, and some drinks.

16. The water in heating pipes remains clear; pitting corrosion of the interior is little. That means energy savings.

17. AL-water leads to energy and wellness in humans and animals. It increases the stamina.

18. The information stored in the drinking water from chemistry and pharmacy is cleared. So, the pollutant frequencies from birth control pills, cytotoxic drugs, beta-blockers, corticosteroids, hormones, plant poisons, fertilizers, and other toxins are rendered harmless.

19. Aqua Lyros water supports the supply of the body cells with nutrients and promotes the disposal of waste products and toxins.

20. The daily drinking of AL-water and repeated weekly bathing gently cleanses the cells and intercellular spaces of heavy metals and other pollutants.

21. The bath water keeps warm longer. There will be no fatigue as it is usually the case in hot baths with plain water.

22. If cows drink Aqua Lyros water, they are more resistant and give more milk. The liquid manure hardly smells. It can be worked better and has a higher fertilizer value.

23. With AL-water, yeast dough rises better. Concrete is firmer. Foods keep fresh longer.

24. Effective Microorganisms (EM) can develop better.

25. Aqua Lyros water achieves better results in fish breeding.

26. The skin does not dry out and feels softer.

27. The hair is soft and yet very strong. We do not need setting lotions.

28. Prof Korotkov has certified the Aqua-Lyros water health benefits.

29. Tea, coffee, and other hot drinks taste better.

30. There are much less aggressive bacteria in Aqua Lyros water.

Experience with the Aqua-Lyros system

As is well known, everything is called into question what is opposed to specific commercial interests. Although, Peter Gross's technology counteracts the bottled water sales, it won 2007 the gold medal at the world's largest International Exhibition of Inventions in Geneva.

In May/June 2009, Dr. Konstantin Korotkov, professor of the State University at St. Petersburg examined three subjects who for five days drank water, which had been activated with Aqua-Lyros. He ascertains reinforced bio-energetic fields of the subjects (www.korotkov.org). Strong energy fields affect the whole organism positively. They form the basis for health and well-being. They also contribute to a spiritual development that our more and more desolate world desperately need. We would also need some enlightened politicians in governments, also more eager and upstanding citizens and less passive and lethargic ones.

From this potential spiritual cleansing process to the real water purification:

The former official expert Rainer J. Ott led on 17.9.2010 a private water test with two processing units in two households. The untreated tap water with a value of about 7,500 Bovis reached with the Schauberger agitator 9,800 Bovis and 24 positive wave-lengths. But the pH of 7.2, the nitrate content of 11 mg and the calcium content of 164 mg the system couldn't change. The situation is different with the Aqua-Lyros system. Compared with the untreated tap water, the energy value has doubled to 16,700, the nitrate value lowered to 6 mg, the calcium value to 113 mg. The pH value changed with 7.4 in the alkaline range. The positive frequencies reached the detectable maximum of 36 positive wavelengths.

Chlorine test report for GIE® activator, the predecessor of the enhanced Aqua Lyros®, by Bernd Bruns in *Naturheilforum Wiesbaden*, December 2007: A chlorine solution (0.01%) with a strong chlorine odor as found in swimming pools, was led via pm (4 bar) through the GIE device and then tested for its chlorine content.

It was no smell of chlorine or chemically chlorine detected. Certain hazardous chemicals are inactivated by the GIE cartridge clearly by intermolecular structural changes.

http://www.naturenergie-leben.de/seiten/aqua-lyros-aktivator.html

Following some personal testimonials of users of the Aqua-Lyros activator:

M. and C. Krumbiegel praise the soft, pleasant taste. Despite regular maintenance and cleaning, a fungus-like surface had formed on the rubber seal. That was dissolved after only four days of daily using the over the bath mounted system. It was completely gone after a few more days.

Gerd Blohm describes the water that runs through the new Aqua Lyros generation as silky smooth and voluminous. The formation of bubbles (oxygen) in the glass is unrivaled.

Jürgen Schmidt and his family like the taste of the water so much that they drink more than ever. It tastes entirely different. The man who installed the unit, immediately asked for the phone number of the Gross family! In the aquarium, the algae infestation was diminished. Even the flowers and plants do great with the AL-water. In the bath, it stays warm longer. That was the first difference I noticed while bathing in the water from the preceding model. With regular tap water, I had to let in more hot water two to three times. The device saves me extra energy.

Susanna Blechschmidt had 30 years problems with dry skin. Since she bathes in water that has been activated by the Aqua Lyros device Helena, she is every time enormously refreshed. Her skin is much smoother. Also, her formerly dry, flaky scalp is silken.

The cells no longer detach themselves from their composite cell, but stick together well. The pleasantly soft-tasting water reminds her of a bubbling mountain spring. *I feel so refreshed that I always strike on ideas that I had never before.*

In Portugal, I tested the Athena activator. This small device was developed as a travel set or for the kitchen and shower. Renate Janzen used it in her bathtub. She made her tea before only with water from plastic bottles. AL-vitalized, she now likes the water that has no more chlorine taste. Anna and Delio Vaz Velho live in an apartment in Tavira. The municipal water is softer with the Aqua-Lyros system. Hair and skin feel softer than before.

In addition to health care, there is another good reason for purchasing the device. It is not necessary to hauling of the bottled water, and the costs amortize in 3 to 4 years. If you are in the habit of drinking Elsenham water for about €10 per liter, you'll manage the payback in 3 to 4 months. But it is far more important to avoid health problems by the unintended side effects of chlorinated water. The result is namely a toxic waste (THMs), which can lead to damage to the nervous system and muscles and loss of consciousness. Also, the byproduct chloroform is suspected of causing cancer. The chloramines also have an allergenic effect. With the Aqua-Lyros activator, we acquire a device for maintaining our health.

The lime content of municipal water in Spain is considerable. Therefore, a friend bought an extra-large unit from the first generation for his 1,200 square meter property.

Previously, every three weeks the coffee maker had to be descaled. K.-D. Kneupper wanted to fill his pool with the same healthy water. However, all the pipes leading to the pool were now completely decalcified. The pool had to be re-filled with clean water. Descaling the coffee machine was not necessary anymore. The previously unpalatable chlorine contaminated water could now be drunk.

In the short time of the tests, hardly any successes in the physical condition can be detected. Especially since in the Algarve we are spoiled by our energy and light giver. When the sun shines, we usually feel well.

I tested the Athena system with cistern water. It showed a pH of 7.5. That is remarkable, since the cistern was due to the rainy season more than 80% filled with rainwater, which is known to be in the acid range of 5.6. The hardness was 1.5 on the border between soft and medium, chlorine 0, lead neg., pesticides neg., nitrates 0.5 mg, nitrites 0.015 mg, bacteria 0.

The issue of water hardness is, however, controversial. Many authors consider hard water as harmless. Three studies seem to confirm this assumption. All have found an association between magnesium deficiency in the water and gastric or esophageal cancer and liver damage. The latter is, according to Mark Howarth and his British fellow researchers caused by the consumption of alcohol in conjunction with soft water and magnesium deficiency (2012).

Hui-Fen Chiu and his Taiwanese team make a high nitrate content responsible for gastric cancer in a magnesium-free water. Yen Hsiung Liao and his also Taiwanese colleagues suggest that trihalomethanes in drinking water still rises the risk of developing esophageal cancer in magnesium-poor water (2013).

We know that gastric and esophageal cancer is more than twice as common in men. The same applies to liver damage. We also know that men eat fewer fruits and vegetables. So they lack vitamins and minerals such as magnesium. Does this mean that if these men drink hard water, they had a chance, still to get some magnesium? On the other hand, when we drink revitalized water, we minimize the cancer risk factor Helicobacter pylori infection. Another risk is a lack of raw food as well as too much of sausage, meat, and tobacco. The Portuguese people often suffer from stomach cancer. Though organic fruits and vegetables grow extensively all over the country, the people eat less of it and lots of sausages. Even in restaurants, salad and vegetables are often only a garnish.

The following chapter is to bring clarity to why hard water does more harm than good. Only light water detoxifies the body and prevents deposits, cancer, heart and kidney disease. In addition, it has a pleasant taste. Especially hot drinks taste better. In soft water, also the flavor of tea and coffee can unfold better. Also, the annoying descaling of coffee machines and faucets is no longer required. With soft water, we also have less work with washing and cleaning and are clear-headed.

Deposits, cancer, kidney and heart disease by the use of drinking water

For 12 years, the hydrologist Prof Luis-Claude Vincent examined, on behalf of the French government, the quality of tap water of various French cities. He could prove a strong link between drinking water and the health and the death rate of the population. His studies showed that in areas with particularly hard, high mineral water, the number of cardiovascular diseases was significantly higher than in areas with soft, low-mineral water.

In areas where the water is still pure, there is almost no disease, especially hardly any cancer or heart attack.

Prof Vincent considered the essential importance of drinking water in its capacity as a solvent for the detoxification and elimination of urinary excreted substances. In addition to the chemical analysis, physical measurement values play a role, e. g., the electrical resistance and the conductance of the water. Soft water cleanses the body, hard water slags it and makes you sick. Vincent created a scale that ranges from diseased to healthy biological water. If H_2O has a resistance of about 6000 ohms and a low electrical conductivity below 200 micro siemens, it contains only a few solutes. *Plose* has a resistance of r = 35,000 ohms (www.acquaplose.it). So it can realize its solution function in the body alright. But in most mineral and drinking waters, the conductance is much higher, and the organism will be burdened. From Vincent's perspective, they are, therefore, totally unsuitable for lasting benefit. Especially newborns suffer from the over-mineralization because their organs are not fully developed. Especially the kidneys are important for water transport (1998). Hence, US mothers give their babies distilled water.

It makes little sense, by the way, to get the values of the tap water from the waterworks because the analyzes relate only to the fountain. The water, that is pressed through long piping, lowers its resistance and thus its purity.

The opinion, the more minerals dissolved in a water the higher is its quality, is widespread. But the body cannot properly metabolize inanimate, as not via solar plant synthesized minerals. They lead to deposits in the connective tissue. This calcification impede the free metabolism between blood vessels and cells and can, therefore, lead to cell degeneration ergo to cancer. This can be illustrated using the example of the potassium sulfate (515 E). Potassium sulfate is the potassium salt of sulfuric acid. The food industry employs E515 as an acidity regulator. Usually, it is used for drinking water and as an additive in soft drinks. It is made by combining potassium chloride and sulfuric acid under the effect of heat by reacting with each other. The result is a colorless crystalline powder, which is only moderately soluble in water. Although the cleavage of this compound metabolizes potassium, but the sulfate remains as free radical and reacts uncontrolled in the body. Curiously, the consumption of inorganic salts cause a lack of minerals and vitamins. This also applies to synthetic vitamin or mineral supplements and drugs. This does not include the Schüßler salts as the body can absorb and use them due to their potentiation. In order to prevent the formation of slag, it is best to avoid ready-to-eat meals with long content lists.

Soft water also counteracts the drying out of the body because it releases the waste from the connective tissue. If we flush out these deposits, the pure soft water can penetrate the cells through the osmotic pressure. With this vital wet, we increase the efficiency of the body.

Burggrabe and Strauß hold that hard water stresses the kidneys. For, the excretory organ has to work hard to remove the unusable salts of hard water from the body. In the long run, it promotes the acidification of the cells, since it does not deliver utilizable mineral salts to move the acid-alkaline balance towards a slight basic range.

We can do a **TASTE TEST**. Two days in a row, we drink mineral-rich water. Then two days we drink water low in minerals, such as Glaciar, Black Forest or Lauretana with less than 50 pm (parts per million). Then we drink

28

again the hard water that has previously tasted wonderful. We will be surprised about our disliking it now.

Another taste test I was able to perform along with some guests at Karl-Dieter Kneuppers Spanish property. The water from the tap was unpalatable because of the chlorine-manure-taste. After activation, with the precursor of the Aqua-Lyros unit, the water was smooth and drinkable and has been used in the future for making coffee. A descaling of the coffee machine was not necessary anymore.

Optimal drinking water is lively

In Portugal, we have a great advantage that in addition to the minerals the pH value is listed on all water bottles. Therefore, we are not even tempted to buy the acidic varieties. It will be best if you contact your elected officials so that we can inform us globally! We take our activated cistern water for cooking and tea or coffee. Underway we drink well water low in minerals, possibly neutral or alkaline. In Portugal, we prefer Cruzeiro from the Luso spring, the extremely light *Glaciar* glacial runoff, or the alkaline water from the Serra de Monchique. On the road in L. A., I use to drink the silica-rich alkaline Fiji preferably. At home, I boil tap water that runs through Peter Gross's device, for 5 minutes. It is cheaper and lighter. Hot boiled water is also drunk in Ayurveda for purification and detoxification. Best is several times a day in small sips. And since the scale-forming minerals precipitate, its lower salt content makes boiled water lighter.

Liquids with a pH less than 7 are acidic, the ones more than 7 are basic. Mineral waters should be as neutral as possible be-cause acid decomposes the teeth over time. The addition of CO_2, which forms carbonic acid increases the acidity. In Vincent's times, hydrologists have specified the ideal pH of drinking water with just under 7. But there was still no fast food. Today, our body cells are so acidified that a pH of 9 now may be the optimum value. A daily intake of 2 liters with a weight of 65 kg should enable well-being. Heat, salty food, competitive sports or heavy physical work twice the amount can be appropriate.

If we trip to the nearby good wells we usually take a supply of the water home by filling in our motorhome tank. There are all good wells in various regions, as can be seen from the fact that people often arrive with a lot of cans or bottles.

In his book *Youthing*, my Down Under living colleague Harald W. Tietze has brought attention to the worldwide problem of acidic mineral waters. He tested 10 Australian ones: Only two are neutral or alkaline (pH 7 and above). One is with 4.1 extremely acidic. Therefore, the researcher, known for his book *Kombucha: The Miracle Fungus,* developed a simple device that allows any water to get on one side in a highly alkaline range. On the other side, the acidic water can be used for plants. However, it is somewhat cumbersome to use and, as in distilling, the room is always damp. It could, however, be used outdoors. I reached deeper into my pockets and got the water activator from Peter Gross. It ensures a pH of 7,5 but without the work and maintenance. Along-side it deletes the pollutant frequencies via extreme turbulence.

Artesian spring water matured more than 150 years. Levitating it still bubbles in 3,000 meters height from the ground. It is particularly invigorating and healing. Such mature waters have very own patterns or frequency electromagnetic oscillations.

Particularly vivid or even higher vibrating are the so-called light or love waters such as the light waters of the French Lourdes, Portuguese Fatima or Italian Montichiari. The spring water from Lourdes has already led to about 7,000 medically recognized cures.

While exploring these light waters, the Italian scientist Enza Ciccolo found that the Lourdes water includes the whole light spectrum. In it, bacteria and other microbes lost their aggressiveness. Prof F.-A. Popp and other quantum physicists found that the biophotons, thus the smallest units of light in these waters, harmonize the body and bring it into a higher vibration.

You may think of it as esoteric boloney. I am open to anything, since I like to experiment myself. When I read long comments in forums, whether anything is a fake or hoax, I give the commentators the advice to dare their own study. For, our experience creates knowledge. That is the true science since it is not based on conflicts of interest or corruption. In this case, the test would not even cost much because the seven vials of the light water from the seven European springs cost only 20 €. Each light water will help for a number of different health problems. A few drops per liter of water is enough.

For example, the *Fatima* Light Water is supposed to connect the body's periphery to the brain (central nervous system) and facilitates the inclusion of other light waters.

The *Lourdes* water is used for clarification, cleansing and restoration at all levels and for activating the metabolism.

The Milan water of *Santa Maria alla Fontana* is known to influence feelings and hormones as well as to act stimulating, strengthening and muscle toning.

The light water from *Montichiari* in northern Italy is good for everything that has to do with nutrition and digestion and affects the hormonal balance and the endocrine system.

The light water from *Medjugorje* in Bosnia is useful to structure, straighten and streng-

then, especially the back and spine, as well as the symmetrical organs.

The Italian *San Damiano* water is said to harmonize, relieve pain and promote sleep.

The Turkish water from *Efeso* should enhance the impact of the remaining light waters and overcome the electromagnetism.

www.lichtwaesser.ch/site/basis.php

A new standard for the assessment of water sat Masaru Emoto by mapping the structures in living water. With the photographed frozen water drops, he showed how in pure spring water the hydrogen fractions chain together with the oxygen to form recognizable structures under the microscope. By contrast, tap water, that is pressed through long pipes, mostly shows no more structure.

The Japanese researcher with his colleagues put a lot of efforts in detecting existing or missing structures in the diverse waters frozen at -5 ° C and photographed at 200 × magnification. In his illustrated books, we can admire downright fantastic crystal pictures of mostly hexagonal stars. They are often designed with rich ornaments as we sometimes see in winter on the window panes. Here, the samples from wells, rivers, lakes or tap waters differ significantly before and after an earthquake. Emoto also informed water samples with positive words or thoughts such as *Love, Thank You, Mother Teresa*, as well as negative words such as *Fool, Dirty, Vicious* or *You make me sick!* The photos of the positively informed samples showed strikingly beautiful crystals. In the negatively informed ones, only fragments of structures were identified. Emoto went a step further, filled water bottles and pinned labels on them. The effect was like the spoken word. When Emoto sonicated water with an edifying, pure music, the structures of the crystals were beautiful, while water exposed to an anapestic beat with a short-short-long rhythm, produced only piteous crystal images (2010).

Do to their long maturing, artesian waters were informed by a wide range of natural frequencies. They have a uniformly distributed structure field. That reflects the balanced energy contributions of the liquid crystals. Also, on the Aqua-Lyros water, about 10,000 material and immaterial, natural frequencies are transmitted, that then harmonizes body and soul. This precious elixir we can easily obtain from the tap and save us hauling bottled water.

If we cannot afford the purchase, we can test wells in the vicinity and use it if appropriate. High-quality waters we best fill in dark glass bottles or terracotta vessels and close them with a cork. Plastic containers are unsuitable because they contain the plasticizer bisphenol A (BPA). Especially babies and small children can suffer damage due to a not yet developed blood-brain barrier.

The above-mentioned water activation technique has the further advantage over the storage of H_2O that it excludes any contamination. The activated tap water eliminates or neutralizes germs and other harmful substances energetically. It clears negative vibrational frequencies and turns ordinary water into a clockwise rotating vitalized water. Also, it has a lower surface tension, is better absorbed and aids digestion. The surface tension of a water of 20° is close to 73 dyn/ cm, at 50° almost 68 73 dyn/cm, and at 80° 62.6 73 dyn/cm, (Wikipedia). Therefore, warm and hot water is good for us.

How does the surface tension work? The electrically charged water particles act like tiny magnets. They stick together with each other and produce a tense surface. This so-called water skin can even carry items such as razors or paperclips, even though they have a greater density than water. Due to the attraction forces between the particles of water, the water skin has a tendency to contract as strained rubber. That gave origin to the term surface tension of water.

Top quality H_2O also offers water-containing fruits. Watermelons usually cost less than commercial varieties of spring water.

Suboptimal liquid in bottles

2012, each German dragged home 137 liters of mineral water. That is a record. Since we sweat the most water while transporting, we need to fill our cells more and more. However, most people prefer carbonated or mixed with fancy flavors waters, usually in plastic PET bottles (polyethylene terephthalate).

With the dissolved carbon dioxide or CO_2 in H_2O, from which the carbonic acid is formed, the taste of poor quality waters can be covered up. Therefore, many people like it better than pure water. It makes more sense to test still water and stay with an agreeable one. Carbonic acid and dissolved CO_2 do not belong in the body. Therefore, we emit it by belching.

We better stay away from sodas and colas, by reason of the sugar content and the synthetic dyes. Even worse is if water or diet soda is sweetened with aspartame. The Monsanto product is one of the most dangerous permitted food substances. In 1970, the neurologist Dr. John Olney discovered that the aspartic acid, which makes up 40% of aspartame, causes pathological changes in the brain of mice. In 1996, he made known the link between aspartame and brain tumors.

In 1986, the psychiatrist Dr. Ralph Woltern found in a 54-year-patient a relationship between her sudden manic episode with insomnia, thoughts escape, irritability and psychomotor acceleration. Especially in summer, she was used to drinking huge amounts of iced tea. Fearing to increase the sugar, she drank tea only sweetened with aspartame. Her condition returned to normal after she returned to the sugar sweetness. It is a fallacy to think that we can lose weight through the use of sweetener. The opposite is the case. Because:

Aspartame excites as E621, the appetite!

In three Californian courts, lawsuits were filed due to health risk against aspartame manufacturers and companies that use it in their drinks and desserts. Aspartame is also known by other names such as AminoSweet, Nutra-Sweet, and Canderel. Not everyone can metabolize Aspartame. Sometimes it leads to cramps, abdominal pain and headache, dizziness, depression unintelligible speech, epilepsy-like symptoms, blurred vision, neurodermatitis, numbness, memory loss, coma, and cancer. Eva S. Scherhammer and her colleagues from the Harvard Medical School in Boston did a cohort study. In 22 years, they researched 77,218 women and 47,810 men and identified in 339 participants leukemia, in 285 bone marrow cancer and in 1,324 lymphoma (2012). Only a single portion of diet soda increases the risk of developing Hodgkin's disease and melanoma. Aspartame also worsens symptoms of ADD, Alzheimer's disease, chronic fatigue syndrome, depression, diabetes, MS, lupus, and rheumatism. Soft drinks are also associated with a higher risk of stroke in women (Eshak 2012).

Since aspartame mimes conditions such as lupus, MS and chronic pain and leads to cancer, interviews with people who had experienced a spontaneous or miraculous healing, interviews would be insightful. Because, if they had changed their diet, it might be no longer a miracle.

Especially dangerous are the sweetened beverages by Monsanto in the summer when the temperature exceeds 30° C.

The methanol in aspartame alters to formaldehyde and then to formic acid or methane.

The latter acid leads to metabolic acidosis. The ex-minister of war Donald Rumsfeld asserted in the transitional government under Reagan the approval of the controversial sweetener. The idea is obvious: a chemical weapon. The chemical company, where Rumsfeld worked before joining the caste of politicians had been taken over by Monsanto. Is Monsanto waging a war with genetically modified food and poisonous sweeteners against the overpopulation? And what would the responsible citizen think about the fact that the manufacturer of the sweet poison is funding the American Diabetes Association? And two of Monsanto's leading people received the World Food Prize 2013!

You may think, what could that bit of diet coke hurt me? But like I said if you think you'll lose weight you are on the wrong track. Here is the proof for the paradox that we even gain weight:

Feijó Fde M and his Brazilian colleagues fed 29 rats for 12 weeks yogurt with aspartame and sugar. They found that the rats fed the sweetener gained with the same number of calories more than the animals fed with sugar. The researchers suggest that a decrease in energy consumption or increase in fluid retention might be involved (2013).

The Neurosurgeon Russell L. Blaylock detected that aspartame and monosodium glutamate (E621, also declared as yeast extract, flavoring, seasoning and broth), cause serious chronic neurological disorders. They are responsible for countless symptoms and diseases such as epilepsy, MS, Parkinson's, Alzheimer's, blindness, brain, skin overgrowth, depression, damaged short-term memory, intelligence weakness. In the US, consumer groups have set up a hotline for aspartame victims.

The sweet leaf extract Stevia is a healthy alternative to artificial sweeteners. Recently, it has been approved as a food in Germany. In Japan, half of the food and drinks are sweetened with Stevia for many years. In USA, you can buy it as a dietary supplement for a long time. Due to the hitherto longer life expectancy of Japanese nobody could claim Stevia can be a health problem. Despite the two recently published studies that aspartame is carcinogenic and runs an increased risk for preterm birth, the European Food Safety Authority (EFSA) sees no reason to alter the current application of the artificial sweetener aspartame! Fortunately, we can still decide for ourselves as competent consumers!

We are better no longer distracted by issues such as engineered pandemic or terrorist threats. Are we better active and prevent serious threats that are secretly implemented quietly, such as foodstuff directives. We don't want to be regulated and would rather decide ourselves what to eat and what not. We also want to choose our means of transportation.

In chapter *FREE ENERGY FOR FREE PEOPLE*, we can inform us about some existing environmentally-friendly drive types. It is best to start petitions or sign already started ones. We are the people!

In his book, *Wasser, die gesunde Lösung* the physician Faridun Batmanghelidj pointed out that diseases are thirst signals of the body. It needs pure water. Unlike camels who have a series of physiological adaptations that allow them to withstand half a year without water, we cannot be without it for more than a week. Cola, soda, juice, beer, coffee and black tea is not a substitute for our most important resource. They even dry out the body, as the substances admixed to water reduces its ability to dissolve. The view of the Iranian doctor based on observation is controversial.

That a glass of water, with which the tablet is swallowed, should be the true medicine, may not suit the prevailing medical operation.

Simple solutions are bad for business. The disease industry flourishes from complicated and costly diagnosis and in the end the incorrect treatment of the symptoms.

On the trail of the best mineral waters

According to § 2 of the natural mineral water regulation, mineral water must come from underground springs protected against contamination. It may be changed only marginally in its composition. But tests in 2011 cannot affirm the original purity of the mineral waters. Clean and natural is different. The degradation products of pesticides from agriculture were in many places penetrated to the deepest depth and exist there as residues.

It would be better for the environment if we ceased to use bottles, by activating our tap water. If you still opt for dragging water, in terms of environmental protection, you better buy local spring water in glass bottles. That Confirms the Swiss study *Ökobilanz Trinkwasser - Mineralwasser*: When we drink 1 liter of bottled water from abroad, we burn up to 0.3 liters of oil. In particular, the transport consumes up to a thousand times more energy than the distribution of the same amount of tap water. Since water distributors are more and more selling their water in plastic bottles, piles of rubbish outgrow. The ideal would be to protect the water from light in dark bottles because the quality remains long. Optimum protection of the bio photons offers bottles of violet Miron glass for sensitive products. They cost about € 3, - per liter bottle. But you have to order bottles, other containers or dishes for a total of € 100: www.miron-glas.com

It is not so easy to figure out the best water. The tests are also a bit tricky. Sometimes, I wonder whether everything is done properly. In July 2011, *Ökotest* tested water without gas. The popular water of the St. Leonhard spring appeared deficient. *Ökotest* measured only the chemical composition and not the ethereal range. In July 2013, *Ökotest* tested the mineral water from the St. Leonhard spring as excellent.

The results and conclusions of the *Stiftung Warentest*, which tested still mineral water on 6-28-12, are not logically from the health point of view. Waters containing few minerals were evaluated as bad, although these cleanse the body better and burden it less. The more minerals and carbon dioxide water contains the less active it is cleansing.

According to Vincent, the mineralization of the blood leads to viscous blood, ergo, to thrombosis and cancer! That was due to a reduction of the resistance in the blood, which is caused by the excess of mineral salts. In *the* July 2013 *Ökotest*, 75 mineral waters have been tested with little gas. Here is a selection of allegedly *very good* varieties: *Gerolsteiner* medium, *Staatl. Fachingen* medium, *Rosbacher* medium, *Rheinfelsquelle* medium, *Tönissteiner* medium.

In March 2013, the test consumer magazine *60 million de Consommateurs* and the nongovernmental organization *Fondation France Libertés* reported on the results of 47 mineral waters from French supermarkets. Every fifth mineral water bottle contained residues of drugs and weedkillers (e. g. atrazine). All in all, the researchers discovered 85 substances that have no place in the water. Also, the popular varieties *Volvic* and *Vittel* were affected. In the *Céline, Cristaline, Saint Amand, Mont Roucous, St-Yorre* and *Salvetat* are residues of the breast cancer drug tamoxifen. In *Hepar* and *Saint Amand*, testers found traces of the blood circulation promoting drugs buflomedil and naftidrofuryl. In eight out of ten samples, were at least one pollutant. In chapter *What to do about the forced medication from the tap?* you can read again about how the harmful substances get into the water.

Even if there is no acute health risk due to low levels of pollutants, the constant accumulation in the body can still be questionable. In addition, small amounts can be dangerous for babies and toddlers. After all, the result of the study is a further incentive to acquire a system that purifies the water and makes germs harmless.

Expensive is not always better; this also applies to bottled water. That is the result of a survey *Stiftung Warentest* in July 2011. The testers took 30 varieties in plastic bottles under the microscope. Their conclusion: Economical drinking means high-quality drinking. Expensive precious waters often disappoint. *Apollinaris* contained in all of the five tested bottles bacteria though not harmful for adults. *S. Pellegrino* from Italy contains a lot of sulfates and the highest uranium and radium values. Water in PET bottles often tastes of lemon and fruity-sweet due to acetaldehyde. That originates from the production of PET bottles. The warmer, brighter and longer water stores in plastic bottles, the more acetaldehyde goes into it. Although it is poor taste, it suppose to be safe. However, we can read the many harmful effects of accumulated acetaldehyde in the liver at Wikipedia. This biochemical compound forms protein structures in the liver that activate macrophages there. These white blood cells secrete substances which alter other liver cells: the fat storing ito cells. These form then increased collagen, which promotes the development of liver cirrhosis. Also, acetaldehyde leads to increased formation of oxygen radicals. Those damage cell membranes, making them perish. At the Goethe University in Frankfurt, the ecotoxicologists Martin Wagner and Jörg Oehlmann noticed a massive estrogenic contamination of bottled water. The hormone activity in PET bottles was twice as high as in glass bottles (Wagner and Oehlmann, 2009, 2011). The researchers had not expected to find such a massive estrogenic contamination in food subjected to strict controls. From a hormonal point of view, they found that mineral water has the quality of sewage plant water.

www.muk.uni-frankfurt.de/38673393/047

In a cohort study at the University of Duisburg, from 2000 and 2002, researchers measured the concentrations of 35 PCBs and dioxins in the blood of 232 pregnant women and later in breast milk. Seven years later, through questioning, it appeared that with overburdening of endocrine disrupting chemicals feminized behavior in male offspring was observed (Winneke 2013). I always thought homosexuality arises from alternating gender in reincarnation, e. g., if we leave the body before or during puberty.

Mineral water without gas

Saskia Jessen is rated as good water with a pH of 7.7. Total dissolved solids 299 mg/l, but it is unsuitable for preparing baby food. It can be prepared with the also as okay rated *Carat* (Fläming Felsenquelle). It has a mineral content of 277 and a pH of 6.6. Volvic was graded satisfying to acceptable; pH 6,5, ashes 150. It is like the as good rated *Vio* Lüner Quelle with a pH of 7,1 and a mineral content of 262 and the satisfying *Vittel* (pH 7,3, ashes 510) not suitable for preparing baby food. The Austrian *Vöslauer* water is because of the high radium-226 content of 47.0 mBq improper for baby food. It is graded as acceptable, has a pH 7.1, TDS 663 mg/l.

Carbonated mineral water

Compared with still waters, those with dissolved CO_2 are consistently in the acidic range. Some of these waters should be suitable for preparing baby food. But we know that dissolved CO_2 does not belong in the body, certainly not in the toddler's body. If the tap water were extremely loaded, I would choose light natural spring waters. But in the long run a water activation system is more economical.

Artificially flavored water varieties

For health-conscious people artificially fla-vored waters are even more critical than the carbonated. The crisp apple on the label, the plump cherry, tangy lemon and ripe straw-berry suggest to the consumer pure nature. Only in the small print we get to know of the artificial apple, cherry, lemon or strawberry flavor. As so often in the food industry, the consumer has been brazenly misled. *Stiftung Warentest* evaluated 25 water brands with a flavor. Not a single water in the test contains a wholly-owned fruit flavor. Except for three waters in the flavors of lemon and lemon-lime, all are tasting flavored and only fruit-like. The fact that these acids attack the enamel is known.

None of the tested waters are good, six are even inadequate. Although the providers ad-vertise with fruits, in fact, the consumer is usually deceived only with fantasy flavors. In three of the waters, the auditors found in the post-test even carcinogenic and germ cell-damaging benzene. This liquid organic com-pound occurs in the presence of the anti-oxidant ascorbic acid from the aromatic preservative benzoic acid. However, since none of the waters contained both substan-ces, the testers astonished the detection of benzene in three drinks with cherry flavor. Benzene is also used for the production of important industrial chemicals, such as ethyl-benzene, found in plastics. But in soft drinks benzene has no place as in food in general.

The water sommelier Martin Riese tasted aroma waters. Skeptical at first, but in the end, he found one without sugar that tastes fresh and not artificial: *Apollinaris, Lemon*. But better is, we flavor our drinks ourselves. We pour activated or 5 minute boiled Adam's ale in a carafe. We add a dash of fruit juice, fruit pieces, ginger, anise or mint and a few drops of Stevia or Xylitol as a natural swee-

tener. Sugar is not only fattening, but also disease-causing, because it increases fermen-tation in the gut. That creates fusel alcohol, CO_2 gas, and methane gas. So we can, with-out ever having a sip of alcohol, barter for a fatty liver or a brandy nose; as well as para-sites, because fungi love sugar. The toxic metabolites lead to inflammation because the organism will burn them. Tooth decay, bar-ber's itch, hay fever and asthma are common consequences. Less well known is that high sugar intake can lead to osteoporosis. Be-cause the body needs to break down sugar and calcium which it gets from the bones.

Lemonade with Cranberry Juice

Baby water for preparing baby food

Water for the preparation of infant formula must meet particularly strict conditions. Since mothers usually have to save money, and the drinking water regulations are any-how strictly complied with the limits for pollutants, in most areas 5-10 minutes boiled tap water is the better solution for small children. Some carbonated waters are offered as baby water, but dissolved CO_2 I would not consider suitable. The same applies with a high mineral content such as *Evian* from the Chachat spring with 506 mg/l. The pH-neutral still water is rated inadequate but suitable for baby food! The barely sufficient rated *Volvic Naturelle* (pH 6.5, minerals 150) without carbonic acid is also a baby water.

Unsuitable for preparing baby food

The *Danone Hayat* from Turkey with a pH of 7.1, total dissolved solids 202 mg/l and the Greek *Korpi* (pH 7.4, 415 TDS) are declared to be inferior and unsuited for preparing baby food. The same applies to the as good to sufficient rated *Gerolsteiner Naturell* (pH 6,8, minerals 862 mg/l). Most waters not suitable for babies contain germs. This is not a problem for healthy people. But for babies or the elderly and sick, the water should be boiled. As long as no pathogens are present, the germ content is admissible.

According to the German drinking water ordinance following maximum values for chemical elements must not be exceeded:

Sodium	20 mg/liter
Nitrate	10 mg/liter
Nitrite	0,02 mg/liter
Fluoride	0,7 mg/liter
Sulfate	240 mg/liter
Manganese	0,05 mg/liter
Arsenic	0,005 mg/liter
Uranium	0,002 mg/liter

http://www.gesetze-im-internet.de/bundesrecht/min_tafelwv/gesamt.pdf

Pure luxury: The world's costliest waters

In sports, it is regarded that for those who train harder and are promoting the most, wins. For the water Olympics, seems to apply: Who filters the most and shines with gilt, snatches the gold medal. For, the expensive bottled water with the sonorous name Bling H_2O was allowed to cream several times in Berkeley Springs International Water Tasting. The dissolved with 140 mg solutes light, and a pH of 7.66 slightly alkaline Tennessee water was nine times filtered before filling into the precious bottle, encrusted with Swarovski crystals.

However, in 2012 won Claire Baie, a cut-price brand from Wisconsin the gold medal at the largest public water tasting in the world, as in 2006 and 2001. Of course, for the cost of less than one euro per liter of pure, deionized water, we cannot expect any decoration. Nonetheless, in this chapter we want to turn back to those bottles waiting to be bought by the ones who consider €100 as peanuts.

The most expensive water in the world, *Rokko No Oishii Mizu,* costs on site, in the Rokko Mountains in Japan, less than €1. In the Adlon Hotel in Berlin, this elegant water is served for €124. It's not even particularly light because it contains 83 mg of hydrogen carbonate, 24 mg calcium, 6 mg magnesium and 18 mg of sodium. The pH I couldn't get anywhere. Better take a test strip along.

OGO, the water from the Netherlands, has a pH of 6.4 and 300 mg solutes. It should be very invigorating because of its high oxygen content of 200 mg/l. That involves for the connoisseur to dig deep into his pocket; it costs €35.

On the largest island of Australia, only 0-600 particles per cubic centimeter of the air were measured. City air contains 10,000 to 300,000 ppm. From here, comes the certified unloaded Tasmanian rainwater *Cape Grim*. It is so pure that an ice cube would defile it and costs €35.

Veen, the water from Finland, has 140 mg solutes, a pH of 6.6, and you can order it in every 5-star hotel in the world for €31.

Between Argentina, Chile and Tierra del Fuego, springs forth the southernmost mineral water in the world. The *Lauquen* spring lies 533 meters deep under the mountains. The water of the pristine nature of Patagonia has a pH of 7.2 and 163 mg total dissolved solids. We have to pay €28.

The *King Iceland Cloud Juice*, present in the media and made of 9,750 drops of the rainwater from Tasmania, is available for €26 a bottle. It is very light and soft (less than 50 mg of solutes). The pH is 7.3. The Aussi water is one of the cleanest in the world.

In exclusive hotels, restaurants and spas, we can buy a bottle of thawed glacial ice off the coast of British Columbia in Canada for €25. *10,000 BC* is one of the purest waters in the world. It has only about 7 mg of solutes and a pH of 6.4.

Originating from the South African wine region Paarl, the *Cape Karoo* water has a pH of 7.2 and contains 442 mg solutes. € 23.00.

The old pure *Elsenham* water is bottled by an artesian spring north of London. In addition to the extravagant patent lock, the water has a pH of 7.6. TDS 400 mg/l. The 0.7 liter bottle can be bought for € 6,30.

With a superb calcium magnesium ratio (Ma 59,4 mg/l Mg 25,6 mg/l) shines the Spanish spring water *Solan de Cabras*. It rests and matures about 400 years underground and takes very slowly minerals in order to come to the surface at a constant temperature of 21° C. 260 mg/l solutes, pH 7.7. It can be ordered on the internet for 4.90.

With a pH of 7.8 and 140 mg of dissolved solids, *Finé* gushes from an underground hot spring in Japan. It contains 81.5 mg silicon.

The 720 ml bottle is available for around €5.

For half price, we get an even higher portion of skin and hair fortifying silicon (85 mg) from an artesian well in the Fiji Islands. The *Fiji* water is filtered by a volcanic rock. It has a pH value of 7.5 and 210 mg/l solutes. We can order online a ½ liter bottle for €2,45.

420 Below rises 200 meters deep on the peninsula Banks in New Zealand. It contains 115 mg of dissolved solids and has a pH value of 7.8. 0.42 liter we can buy from €5.

Heartsease, the H$_2$O against lovesickness of the Radnor Hills of Wales shines with a pH of 7.9. It contains about 300 mg solutes.

As the water of the heart, *Llanllyr* water also stems from Whales. It can be bought for €4 per liter. It is acidic with a pH of 5.9; TDS 111 mg. They include manganese and zinc. These trace minerals are needed for high alcohol consumption but are better absorbed from nuts, green leafy vegetables, cheese, seafood, and giblets.

Voss, the precious water from southern Norway, is pure; it contains only 22 mg/l total solutes. Designed by Calvin Klein, the bottle stands out. The pH is 6.4. For one liter, we have to pay €4.99.

The Welsh water *Tau*, sold by Ty Nant, comes in an award winning clear, minimalist modern glass bottle. The pH of the noble wet is 6.8, the solutes 165 ml/l. It is often offered in a 12-tray for € 38.28. Individually, you can order the 0.7 l bottle online from €3,30.

The legendary mineral water *San Pellegrino* rises 700 meters underground in the Lombardy Alps; pH 5.4, solutes 930 ml/l. We can order the 0.7 l bottles online for a liter price of €1,47. In the restaurant, a bottle costs about €5. For babies and toddlers, the water is unsuitable because of the high uranium content of 4-8 micrograms per liter. PET bottles are suboptimal due to production costs and acetaldehyde (sweet and sour taste).

Owned by the Elisabethen Quelle Hesse, *LIZ* water comes in an elegant carafe with a spout. It is available in 0.75 and 0.35 liters. Some people may buy the twelve 0,7 l bottles only because of the design. The price, €17 per case, seems worth it. Suitable for athletes is the excellent ratio of calcium and 102 mg/l magnesium 35,4mg/l.

From the hundreds of brands of mineral water next the especially light, basic and acidic ones.

Extremely light, alkaline, and acidic water

The energetic charged precious *Glaciar* water makes a thirst for more. The pure glacier water gushes out 1,400 meters above the sea level in the protected Parque Natural da Serra da Estrela in the heart of Portugal. It has a lot of awards and it is certified by the US Food and Drug Administration as a quality food. With a TDS of 16 mg (8 mg silicon), it belongs to the lightest waters. Equally light are *US Rain* (TDS 1.5, pH 9), *Sparkletts* (TDS 18, pH 7.3) and *Philippine St. James* (1 TDS, pH 7.2). Almost all the analyses in the book obtain from the following link:

www.mineralwaters.org Alas, after more than 17 years, the website closed. Why? Were too many crucial new analyzes on the horizon? One of the bad news I found here:

www.strahlentelex.de/uran_Mineralwasser-Messwerte.htm

Glaciar contains 9,40 µg/l uranium and is, therefore, unsuitable for small children.

The Peak value of the basic water has *Aqua Alca* from Bosnia and Herzegovina with a pH of 11.6 (TDS 130 mg/l). It follows the Swedish calcium and bicarbonate-rich *Vilamina* 10.4 (TDS 170). The Brazilian *Ibira* has a pH of 10.03 (TDS 274). The Bulgarian *Gorno Bania* has a pH of 9.7 with borderline arsenic and barium according to drinking water regulations. *Trinity Springs*

from the USA has a pH of 9.6 (TDS 195, 74.6 mg of silica 74, 6, fluoride 3.5). Almost as basic is the *Monchique* Algarve Mountain water with a pH of 9.5 (TDS 300, fluoride 1.2). The five most acidic mineral waters are all from Brazil: *Aqua plus* 4, *Belaqua* 4.08, which is particularly light, *Aqua Cristalina de Anapolis* 4.2, 4.5 and *Aqua Mineral Prata Dovale* 4.5.

You may wonder why I list the expensive water when I could recommend regional wells in order to protect the environment. I hope to reach a wider audience with this comprehensive offer. And, maybe one or the other becomes aware of the drawback of the liberalization of world trade, precisely by reading this.

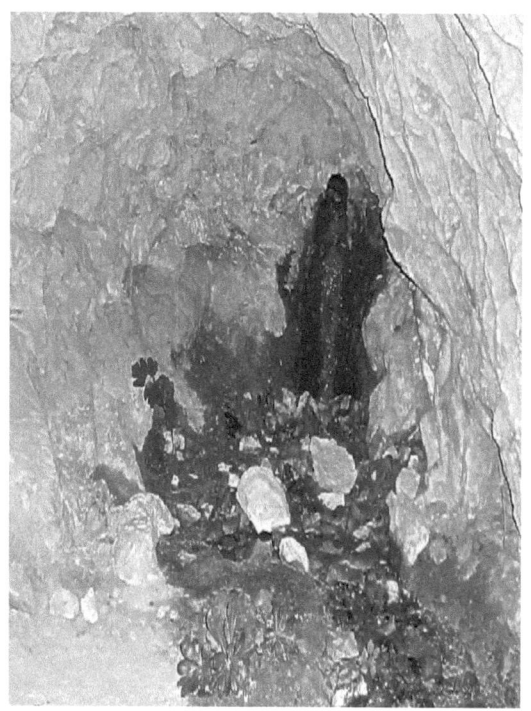

Current limit values of the German drinking water regulations in mg/l

(Source Wikipedia)

Acrylamide	0,0001
Aluminium	0,2
Ammonium	0,5
Antimony	0,005
Arsenic	0,01
Benzo(a)pyrene	0,00001
Benzene	0,001
Lead	0,01
Bor	1
Bromate	0,01
Cadmium	0,003
Chloride	250
Chrome	0,05
Coliform and Clostridium bacteria	0
Cyanide	0,05
1,2-dichloroethane	0,003
Iron	0,2
Epichlorohydrin	0,0001
Fluoride	1,5
Copper	2
Manganese	0,05
Sodium	200
Nickel	0,02
Nitrate	50
Nitrite	0,5
Pesticides and Biocidal, total	0,0005
polycyclic aromatic Hydrocarbons	0,0001
Colony count	100 /1ml
Mercury	0,001
Selenium	0,01
Sulfate	250
Tetrachloroethene and Trichloroethene	0,01
Trihalomethanes	0,05
Uranium	0,01
Vinyl chloride	0,0005
Hydrogen ion concentration (pH)	6,5 – 9,5
Tritium (bq/l)	100

III. WATER AS INTERFACE BETWEEN PHYSICAL AND METAPHYSICAL REALITY

Only a penetrating study by intuitively gifted people can fathom the innermost nature of the life-giving substance, water. Only through a painstaking investigation of the materialized ur-substance, water, will it become possible to show a mentally and physically degenerating humanity the ways which will once more lead us upwards.

(Schauberger 1963, S. 7)

Regrettably, after three generations, the words of the forester, inventor, and scientist have gained even more in importance. In my book *Wasser - Code geknackt?* I have presented my experiments with Ernst F. Braun's water crystal photography. It was then clear to me that H_2O mediates between the worlds. Via microscope photography, we can see the stored messages in water drops.

However, most people have problems with the puzzling phenomena and react with denial and repression. They tend to blank out anything that might jeopardize their worldview. Yet, I understand it as my destiny to investigate the uncertainty until it is cleared. Of course, it also plays a role that on my mother's side, the extrasensory perception is nothing unusual. Ma had second sight from her childhood on. A cousin is active in animal communication; another saw the spirit of her spouse at his funeral leaning on a tree. She and some of her visitors could then hear him as poltergeist or smell his cologne during the following year. My ability of clairvoyance, clairaudience, aura reading, past-life dreams, and psychometric increased in California after quitting eating meats and drinking coffee. I ate almost only vegetables, salad, and fruits. My brother discovered his prophetic potential at age 6. Once he was staying with his handball friends in Paris. They drove around aimlessly, had a drink here and a snack there until they realized that they were hopelessly lost. Suddenly, my brother saw a three-dimensional map of Paris in his mind's eye. On an entirely different way, he led the puzzled driver back to the hotel. What dynamics had made this perception possible?

Water as a mediator between the worlds

Today, physicists and mystics agree that awareness initiates all things. Everything existing is animated and vibrates. All particles act intergalactic, and they contain water. Unconsciously we all communicate with each other, even with animals and plants. Water is the conductor. Plants feel when the leaves of a neighboring plant are cut off. According to a study, the soul energy acts between plants and animals. A measuring instrument was connected to the plant. When next to it living crabs were thrown into a pot of boiling water, it showed excitations in the cellular system.

We communicate unconsciously via our mental radar network with other people. In this soul field, the vibrations take effect. Faraday coined the term field and spoke of the electromagnetic field. In contrast, Sheldrake's morphogenetic fields are a kind of astral memory (Akashic) of non-physical nature. In his view, a field design stands behind each structure, formed for the first time, be it a thought, a fact or a material object. The more often this structure forms, the stronger the morphic resonance. Sheldrake suspected not only the genetic code specifies inheritance. Lessons learned and experiences that are not included in the genes, could be passed on to future generations. A disease, such as a colon tumor, can thus be family correlated. If we recognize the trigger and solve the first conflict that holds advantages for future generations. E. g., if a young man got killed in a car accident, his wife or daughter may have problems to overcome the tragic death. They cannot digest it. It sticks in the morphic memory. The latter helps some species globally implement environmental changes. For instance, horses were injured on barbed wire fences. Since they got used to those fences in some countries, the horses globally ceased to get hurt (Sheldrake 1993).

But how does the mediation between the worlds take place? It is clear that the water is available everywhere; solid, liquid or gaseous. Based on my experience with the excellent universal means for dissolving, storing and transporting I want to unravel the mystery. That involves the just revealed less known ability of H_2O to receive and store the contents of consciousness.

What has telepathy to do with water?

Iron rusts from disuse; stagnant water loses its purity and in cold weather becomes frozen; even so does inaction sap the vigor of the mind.

Leonardo da Vinci

Plato tells us that the Atlanteans should have communicated telepathically. Water was everywhere for the people of Atlantis. Another great thinker, who knew how to use the essential element, was Goethe. He often visited spas because there the heavenly messages flowed better. The latter I noticed when I took baths almost daily in California and had increased extra-sensory perception, prophetic dreams and other psychic phenomena. Frequent bathing, water-rich foods and not eating meat increases the ability of communicating thoughts, feelings and images.

From Emoto's water crystal photography, we know that the water can transfer the vibrations and information of words and thoughts. In 1997, Emoto sent a letter to 500 Hado Instructors in Japan with the following text: *At 2pm on February 2, 1997, I will leave a cup containing the tap water of Shinagawaku on the table in my office. Please transmit your feelings to that water at the same time from all over Japan. Of course, for this water to become clean water, please send „Qi and Soul of Love" and the wish that the water should become clean. Thank you very much.* When the staff saw Emoto's beautiful water crystals, they were overwhelmed and close to tears.

This experiment proves that thoughts can be merged, regardless of their distance. It also suggests that our good words and deeds make water pure and beautiful. Emoto calls this effect on water, the law of sympathetic resonance, Hado. He describes it as the *intrinsic vibration pattern at the atomic level*. The particle physics recognized, however, in 1964 the quarks as the smallest units of matter and as energy. But whether you want to consider the quarks as a mediator between the third dimension of objectivity and the fourth dimension of thought and spirit, is up to you.

Anyhow, physicists and mystics of today agree:

Consciousness initiates all things.

We know about the informing of the water from the homeopathic shaking (succussion). It is so incredibly boundless as if Freddy pours a thimbleful informed water in the Azores in the Atlantic Ocean, blows vigorously via the south and from the Weddell Sea takes a sample. Nevertheless, the water informed by the active substances of the homeopathic remedy can pass on health-giving information to the water in our body cells.

We know from animal communication of our four-legged friend's special mediality. The reason is they are less distracted. Also,

for us humans, telepathy is not necessary since the invention of the telephone. However, we can still test our medial abilities as we set a specific time and date for a person to watch each other. Prior to that, the meditative grounding is recommended.

Meditation: A few deep breaths, feet firmly on the ground. Imagine being a tree. The roots go deep into the ground and absorb the water and nutrients. The leaves blowing in the wind and irradiated by the sun. We can also visualize us in a tube that reaches far up in the sky and until deep into the ground. From above, a glistening light falls down on us, in which we bathe cozily. Then we focus on the person. I performed this exercise during a three-month block seminar with Taryn Krivé, a well-known medium in California. With my mind's eye, I saw that my partner undressed himself a few times. When I then spoke to him, he said: Oh! I was hoping you had not noticed. I had to go to the bathroom a couple of times.

But how do we perceive information from animals? We cannot make an appointment. The more we compose ourselves and adjust us to an animal, the sooner we can develop the ability to clairvoyance, mind reading, and clairaudience, -tasting, and -smelling. Like our muscles, we can train our mediality. Animal communication is a skill that is inherent in all of us, but it must be re-awakened. With our growing expertise, we enrich our lives and living with our animals. Because if we understand what they want from us, we can avoid many misunderstandings.

I exemplify the channelings by my cousin animal communicator Heide Bayer from Eberbach/Neckar (an-edelstein@web.de). My elderly dog Leo suddenly went lame. By a blood test, the vet ruled out an inflammation, made an X-ray appointment and gave me pain pills. Heide offered me the following morning to talk to Leo. She pointed out he may not react right away. I emailed her a 2-week-old photo of Leo. Heide called me around noon to tell me about their conversation. She'd asked Leo about pain. Leo: Sometimes. Heide: But Marianne gives you medications. Huh? Leo showed a wholly surprised face. I had never told him that in the sausage or a piece of cheese was a tablet. Afterward, I always showed Leo the yellow particles I pressed into the goodies and said, Here your medicine.

With the **reading of thoughts**, the mediator asks the animal a question and instantly knows the answer. On Heide's question, what happened, she immediately saw Leo walking backward and another dog she described me as a light brown smaller one with some white on the neck, apparently his girlfriend Mia. Then, Heide suddenly saw something red swoosh passed. Yes, that was probably the always speeding Englishwoman, the only red car in the area. Leo's first dog friend also may have fallen victim to her some 7 years ago. For, every time Leo and Mia rush furiously behind the car; When Shirl rides on horse's back, they remain quiet.

At first, we may not be sure if the data indeed come from animals or are based on imagination. However, telepathically transmitted messages always have typical characteristics. They come spontaneously, and we are totally certain the answers come from the animals or if we receive a message we could not possibly know. In the example, Heide could not have known the information with the red trouble car.

We speak of **clairvoyance** when we see pictures, fragments or image sequences.

Heide further asked, can Marianne do something else to bring you relief? At this time, she saw Leo having fun in a shallow river. Leo used to love water. Heide also smelled the sea water and heard a rustling. We used to take Leo to the river because the area is deserted. Leo was very shy of people and ran away in panic. Therefore, we only took Mia to the ocean. I certainly had a guilty conscience and thought to take Leo on a leash at least in winter to secluded beaches.

Via **clairolfection**, meaning opening up our psychic sense of smell, we get the information in the form of odors.

Another media transmission is the **clairtasting.** If we ask a dog or a cat after the favorite food and there is an intense fishy smell, we can assume that the animal loves fish.

And last but not least, we can obtain information by **clairsentience,** via physical and emotional feelings of the present, past or future physical and emotional states of our pets. We feel on specific topics in the area of the solar plexus between the heart and abdomen. We, therefore, speak of the gut feeling. Does it feel good, relieving, relaxing or do we feel some pressure or node? For example, if we confront strangers, we can ask ourselves: What kind of human is this? How do I feel near to him? Would it be better to stay away from him? The same applies to animals.

But what has telepathy to do with the water? I assume that water or humidity channels thoughts. In other words, water is the medium that directs the energies via duration, extent and spin. That water transmits better than the air we learn when bathing. If we have the head under water, we can hear our roommates speaking in the house.

We know from the homeopathic succussion that the energy or active frequency is still present in the water, even though we are no longer able to prove the matter. Just as the thimbleful of an active substance, makes it from the Azores to the Weddell Sea, consciousness reaches the remotest corner of the world, as explained in the previous chapter.

The transfer of our thoughts, so it seems, we owe the quarks. These tiny elementary particles are energy.

Does telepathy also have to do with the guiding home of abandoned animals? In any case, physicists and mystics agree: awareness initiates all things. Quarks are the intermediaries between the third dimension of objectivity and the fourth dimension of the mind and spirit.

* Our pets are masters of telepathy.

* Mind-reading is best done after a meditation.

* With clairsentience we pay attention to the question of our gut feeling. Do we feel free, relaxed or nervous or depressed?

* Water conducts energy (thoughts, feelings) via duration, extent, and spin.

* We communicate with our mental radar network. We think, and the electromagnetic field carries the vibrations of thought, and the other can receive it.

How do we intercede between the worlds?

One way to connect the material and the spiritual level of existence is via water crystal photography. It demonstrates the intergalactic activity of all particles. Another way of contacting is when we pay attention to the so-called coincidences or miracles. Also, when we center ourselves, we can see miracles. What prevents us? Addictive Substances, violent films, and computer games remove us more and more from our center. Many people barely use their right brain of spiritual thought. The bodily functions concerning we may have come close to our ideal of creation. But as for the spiritual, it is high time that we find our way to the perfect form. Children can help us to stay on course. Their authenticity and impartiality can guide us. We better pay attention to their behavior and their words instead of dismissing them as fantasies. Toddlers who are up to 85% made of water, are mostly still in their midst. They use, such as only one-tenth of mankind both halves of the brain in a balanced way. They are connected to the other side. Some get spiritual help. Others speak to their imaginary friends. They are mostly the souls of relatives who long since had fallen victim to a war or as infants to a vaccine or as fetuses to x-rays or medication.

We can regenerate ourselves and our planet as we focus on our mental computer. By drinking 2 to 3 liters of activated water meditating, living and eating naturally and practice positive imagination, we raise our vibrational frequency. Thereby, we activate our right brain.

Below I bring my second face to your attention, in the hope, some polluters are transformed into conservationists. After all, would we not be more motivated to protect our environment, if we'd have to expect to populate the earth again in another body? You may call me a naive optimist. But would it not be a blessing if irresponsible shipowners stopped to pump tons of their oil sludge into the sea? Or farmers would delight us with organically grown gene-free fruits, rather than pollute our elemental wet.

In the mid-80s, I already talked about my

supernatural experiences. I had often fallen on deaf ears or looked into contorted eyes. In California, however, I regularly met people who entrusted their psychic experiences to me. That may have to do with the upbringing that leads to self-assurance. It could also have to do with the high water consumption of Californians. The water seems to channel the cosmic messages better. Fortunately, the Germans had been brought closer to the metaphysics in the last years.

Water collects information and energy anywhere where it is. Years ago, we still thought the water recirculation was restricted on our planet. Since the press release from NASA, in May 1997, with photos from huge snowballs falling from space, we can assume different dimensions. Just as our body water reacts emotionally to the other body, the water on Earth seems to affect other celestial bodies and vice versa. Since H_2O is able to store information and physical forces, it can also bring messages from the universe. So the healing wet seems to connect the metaphysical and physical world. The subtle element in the water carries our prayers to departed spirits, and the souls send us messages via water.

Lies all truth in the water? Around 60 years ago my grandmother expressed this in the following poem:

Geist der Wahrheit, Licht und Klarheit
Trägst du in das weite Land,
dass verschwinde Nacht und Sünde
und das Einssein wird erkannt.
Höchster Geist, erfülle nun die Herzen,
Tau des Himmels, heile alle Schmerzen.
Der große Tag des Herrn ist nicht mehr fern.

Maria Holschuh

In our first location in California, I realized that the water is our bridge to the ether. There I experienced the most intense phase of psychic experiences. In a small beach community on the Pacific coast piled up the so-called coincidences that Jung called synchronicity. Revealing had been dreaming of past lives and future events. Before, I had only déjà vus of forgotten true dreams. We can recognize them when people, environments or situations are strangely familiar, as if we had experienced it all before. It is best to write down all the dreams so we can confirm the prophetic ones later.

Sometimes, during meditation or just before sleep, a bright light penetrates into my forehead chakra. When this sparkling diamond burst in the third eye, it is as if the water in all cells vibrates. Then a sense of unconditional love and a comforting feeling of security flows through me, which makes me feel One with all creation.

While my maternal relatives have psychic experiences since childhood, they came to me as a toddler and were probably blocked due to many diseases and operations till the end of the 70s. Owing to the regeneration of the research group for Geo-Hydro-biology, my channel had been reopened. Learn more about it in *Wunderwesen Wasser*. At first I was not aware that the spiritual world used me as a channel. One of my earliest media experience I only had recognized as such until much later. It happened during my doctoral studies.

My professor Anitra Karsten had organized a meeting with professors and selected students of gerontology in the Frankfurt Uni tower. We wanted to draw up a petition to establish the *University of the Third Age* and submit them to the then Minister of Social Affairs Armin Klaus. Contrary to my custom, I participated very actively in the discussion and was wondering where suddenly the great thoughts came from. About half of the petition based on my suggestions. I took it home to make it even pass through the channel of the FDP. Mr. Mischnick, the son of a politician, lived in the same house as we did. I asked him to give the petition to his father. A fellow student asked afterward about the details. But it was nothing I could have told her. The whole event was like a dream that I remembered vaguely. I would have liked to repeat the inexplicable spiritual highs and had everything I had done the day before, pass by: Cleaned, fasted, bathed... (?). It was only much later that I realized that an ethereal creature apparently had used me as a medium. The spiritual sometimes intervenes in order to serve as a sound purpose. In this case, they helped to set up the Training Institute for the elderly to live.

Why were my experiences cumulative in Hermosa Beach? I saw ghosts, was shortly paralyzed by my late mother-in-law and had almost daily prophetic dreams, for a period also dreams of past lives. In one of these past-life dreams, I was an English-speaking actor, residing in a hotel. The members of the heavenly orchestra made me meet the Hollywood actor John Hudson. In addition to the soap opera Doctor in General Hospital, he also starred alongside Kirk Douglas in *The Racers* and in many Westerns. As a former lover of Jocelyn Brando, he introduced me to the actor-sister of the famous performer. With her, I met two other actresses who took me to their schools. I tested my talent with Sharon Chatton. She trained her students in Brentwood and Santa Monica. After four weeks, Sharon praised me more than Mariel Hemingway, Peter Lawford, and other established actors. That was all I wanted to know; the talent seems to confirm this earlier life.

That the increased supernatural powers had to do with the water nearby, I realized only later. The ocean was only a few hundred meters away, the pool right outside the house. Since, as usual in America, water and electricity costs were included in the rent, I took almost every winter day, a full bath and ate more fruits and vegetables than ever. With high humidity or the rain we often dream of the deceased.

Goethe afforded many spa treatments because he had noticed that the water keeps the flow of heavenly messages in motion.

He was convinced that his words were words from a higher world. Goethe saw his task, or the heavenly mission to save people from the bonds of earthly entanglements and to show them a way out of the confusion towards freedom. Rather failed? But probably the knowledge of the gist of the matter is not far off.

* Water transmits information from space. Therefore, the extrasensory perception is higher in humidity.

* Drinking living water (2 to 3 l), meditation, positive affirmations, water-rich vegetarian food and avoiding addictive substances raise our vibrational frequency.

* Toddlers who consist of about 80% water, are particularly intuitive. They understand, long before they learn to speak.

* The spiritual world, our deceased or other spirit helpers, still participate in the earth-ly life projects.

* Forgotten prophetic dreams are emerging as déjà vus when the previously dreamed scenes take place in reality.

Water Crystals: language of the souls

Emoto proved the perception and memory ability of the water with the water crystal photography. H_2O receives information or electromagnetic oscillations in the microcosm of the cells and the macrocosm of the planets. If we want to deal with this little-known side of the water, we cannot ignore the research results of Albert Einstein and Max Planck. Looking at the structure of the world and matter, they discovered that there is no matter in itself. All observation objects, every atom and molecule are, therefore, a collection of vibration patterns.

We can assume at present that the whole system of our visible world, from the smallest elementary particles of all visible life on earth to the farthest star, emerged from a universally existing energy field. This quantization and signal processing of energy, momentum, and interacting particle fields are visible through the water crystal photography. Due to the dipole character, individual molecules form themselves to hydrogen bonds and are clustered together. By mutual tightening, the electrical charge differences form hydrogen bonds. They link together as so-called clusters. The binding forces of hydrogen bonds are much less than the binding forces within the water molecule. They can, therefore, easily be assembled and dismantled. Complex molecules can be broken in a split second and rebuilt. This property of unswerving solving and forming leads to the crystal structures in the water drops. Those we can admire in the winter in the frozen state, on the window as snow crystals. What energy is at work? Who brings us the stars from the sky and paints them on the window?

In the following, we want to explore the hidden dynamics behind in the water crystallized subtle vibrations of thoughts and feelings.

Through the experiments with the Swiss water artist Ernst F. Braun I realized who is painting pictures via sound waves or vibrations of writing or color in the water:

Our deceased friends and relatives! Though Mr. Braun does not explicitly suggest this interpretation, he calls the water crystal photos informed by a person's *soul star*.

The idea of interacting souls may seem bizarre. The observation of trance mediums or prodigies, such as Mozart or today Jay Greenberg, can help to understand the concept. As a toddler, Jay wanted a cello by painting it. In a music store, he got a miniature cello and began to play. At the age of 12 years, he had already composed five symphonies. He composed *The Storm* in a few hours. Jay speaks of multiple channels and that the music comes involuntarily. It simply fills his head.

www.wimp.com/musicprodigy

The spirit painter in the video link below is another example of channeling:

www.youtube.com/watch?v=URM8KGpjztE

Shirley MacLaine visited Luiz Antonio Gasparetto at his home in Orange, California, to watch his other-worldly work. Henri de Toulouse-Lautrec came through and said he had her painted before and talked about her former life as a courtesan in Paris. It is no wonder that Shirley received an Oscar nomination for Irma la Douce. My late friend Dr. Ingrid Dennerlein-Barmack also had confirmed the authenticity of the medium. She had translated for Antonio in Brazil. But nobody must believe in the soul or eternal life to be surprised by this film. Luiz paints in a trance old masters. He uses crayons and tubes of paint. The spirit artists use Luiz as a channel to show us: Just see we still exist!

Gasparetto paints at lightning speed without looking. In 2 to 3 minutes, a Modigliani, Renoir, and van Gogh are finished. Luiz is in contact with the painters. He loans them, so to speak, his hands and sometimes feet. We can visit him and buy *his* paintings for a few bucks.

The souls of Dr. Barnard, Dr. Sauerbruch, and other famous surgeons can work through the mind-operators as shown by Oprah Winfrey:

www.youtube.com/watch?v=PNIbvItdjws

Other projects of the spiritual world are in my opinion hypnoses and family constellations. They should help to dissolve entanglement dynamics and to help us better cope with the earthly life.

Equally surprising as channeling old masters are the water crystal photos (WCP) in the following chapter. A few years ago, I realized that there were also art painters at work with my water crystals. My childhood sweetheart, Edmond Dembinski, died some 13 years ago. I had led him to the art. Edi came at age 17

from the hotel management school in Salzburg to my hometown. I believed in his artistic talent and asked him to make an art folder. I went to the Offenbach College of Design with him. The professor liked Edi's work. After a few months of training at the School of wood and ivory in Michelstadt, he began his studies. That was obviously my job, because shortly after we parted. So I think that Edi gave me most of the unusually large number of soul stars. His writing and his graphics are full of signals. They symbolize beauty but are also clear warning signs to protect the environment! My husband's painting Uncle Adolf from Gauting could also have been involved. But since I never met him, I think more of Edi's mother, Wanda von Dembinski, who could paint a portrait in oil with soul in 1-2 hours. Also, I think of my father's friend Joachim Gestering and his

graphically precise, slightly morbid images. Especially since Jochen showed me shortly before his death, the doctoral thesis of his son Johann Joachim: *German Pessimism & Indian Philosophy. A hermeneutic reading.* At that time, I told him about the spirit experience with my great-grandfather who had emigrated to the USA, taken the family name Victor and lived in the Carmel area. My father's grandmother was pregnant from him since Christmas 1901. A young man from the New Apostolic congregation saved the honor of Wilhelmine Meckes, and Maria Hörr came on October 5 as seven months child. The family secret was well kept. The love child was my poetry-writing darling grandmother. And since my probably 1902 to the USA emigrated great-grandfather showed himself to me, I want to find out about my paternal relatives. Since then I wish to get a chance to identify my ancestor in a photo album. Probably he was new apostolic, possibly related to the Meckes family.

Will I ever meet one of those Victors who were said to have settled in the beautiful area around Carmel in California? About four years ago I learned that my mother is related to the Carmel resident Doris Day. This synchronicity asked me to write an autobiographical novel *DORIS DAY AND MY SEARCH FOR RELATIVES.* With that, I expected to find my father's relatives and inform the actress-singer about her Neckar relatives.

Ernst Braun was amazed that from the 22 frozen water drops informed by my signature he photographed 15 *soul stars*. He usually gets 8, sometimes only 4. Incidentally, it was Peter Gross, who introduced me to the water artist's work. He emailed me two water crystal photos of water from the same tap.

The first one was obtained from the ordinary tap water, the second from the water that ran through the GIE activator. It was the previous

model of the Aqua-Lyros device. Today, all apparatuses originally created by the Gross family are the Aqua-lyros models from www.aqua-lyros.de.

People have tried to copy the GIE technology. Buying such a device is wasting money. Only the original water-activator by Peter and Isabel Gross carries out their conception with the perfect technology.

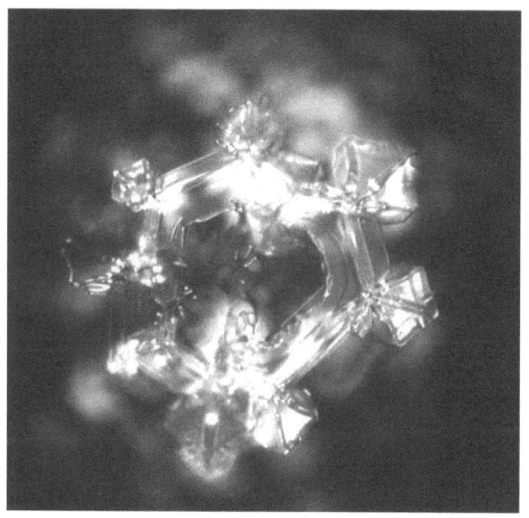

The pictures taken before passing through the device seem like a hopeless mess. They show no crystal formation. The ones taken after running through the activator are clear with a beautiful crystal formation and show a separation. They tell the sorry saga of his genius exploited engineer. I may write a mystery novel about it.

Everyone their own *soul star*

How can we use water as a mediator between the worlds? One concept is to inform and read your water crystal photos. In the Studio for Art and Mystic Ernst F. Braun and his daughter Sarah Steinmann photograph based on the method of Masaru Emoto frozen water drops. This task is mastered only by few intuitive persons. The microscope photography is also a costly endeavor. How the Swiss do their job, remains their secret. You are welcome to assist them with exciting orders.

You might want a soul star from your spouse or the kids. They make unique posters. I even submitted the photo of my cat Max by e-mail. The traditional version is to get a 30 ml glass vial with a plastic cap at the drugstore or pharmacy and fill it with distilled water. We can put the bottle in a child's bed or a dog basket. Who can write his name, simply signs. Best to wrap the bottle in aluminum foil and send in a padded envelope to the Studio for Art and Mysticism. Important: Don't attach labels. If there are several, only markers, such as 1, 2, 3, or A, B, C. We can write down or memorize the numbers matching the name.

Testing of the group dynamic

If we are unsure to remain faithful to a choir, sports club or a political party, we could consult the soul stars. Just take a vial of neutral H_2O to the event. The good spirits can scan the group dynamic vibrations transmitted to the water and surprise us with their water crystals. This way, they can bring some nonbelievers to reflect. And our departed loved ones are anxious to let us know the truth.

We could also let the soul stars tell us, when it comes to the question of joining a residential community. Perhaps the spiritual world would also be inclined to participate in marriage counseling. We put the vial in the center of the family or group circle and ask people to address their questions to the water souls. Mostly fine crystals I would interpret as a *yes*; without crystalline structures, it would be a *no*. With a bit of clairvoyance, we could discover the reasons respective decisions in the water crystal photos.

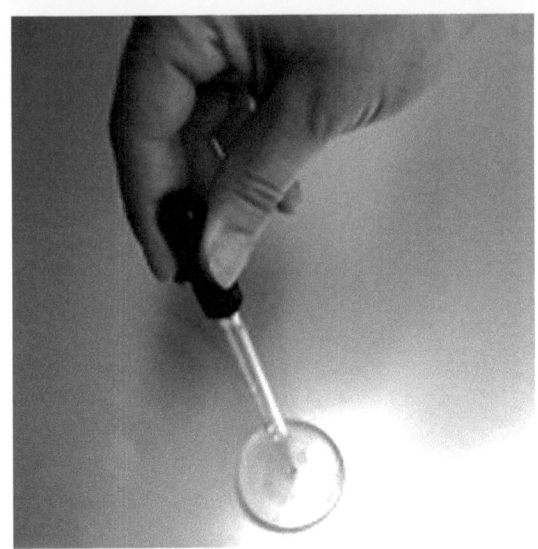

Creating a soul star by Ernst F. Braun

When a vial of distilled H2O reaches the studio, the 22 drops can be at once isolated and frozen. With the symbolic Master Number 22, the artists were always well advised.

Arrives a piece of paper with a signature, E. Braun or S. Steinmann wrap it around a vial with pure water and leave it for 1-3 days. Just as long, they put a bottle with distilled water on the photo. Then they take the drops and freeze them individually in Petri dishes at -30° for a few hours. The tiny ice chunks are then photographed under a microscope at -5°. The artists must wait for the right moment. Out of every drop shapes are seen. WCPs with visible structures are selected and optimized via lighting and color. The forms remain unchanged. Sometimes the photos tell whole stories. To me they were milestones of my life. The messages shown by the artists of this world and beyond are incredible. They are always unique. The superior photo of the series, enlarged or painted, is an original gift. How the Swiss help us to get them we can learn on the Internet: www.wasserkristall.ch

Are soul stars replacing the crystal ball?

We can also generate soul stars by writing down questions under the signature. The advantage over the crystal ball is: when looking at the WCP we have all the time in the world. Often we recognize a message only by repeated viewing. I realized that children are great

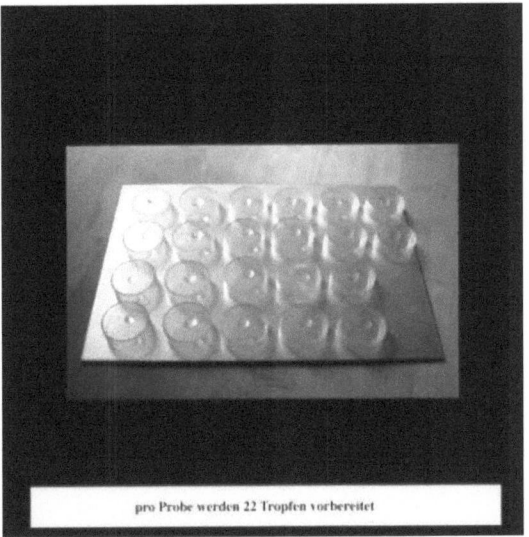

pro Probe werden 22 Tropfen vorbereitet

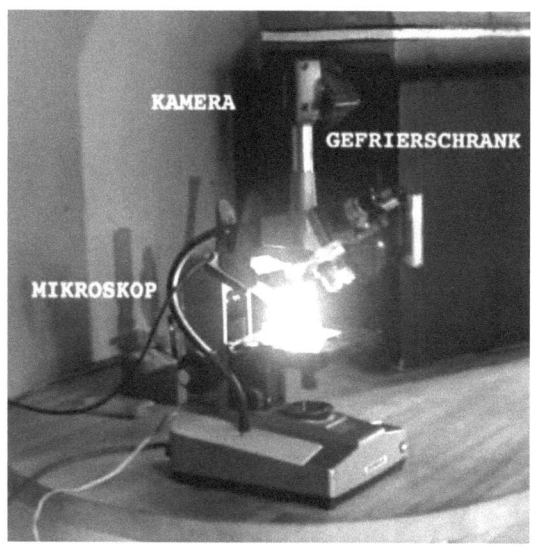

KAMERA

GEFRIERSCHRANK

MIKROSKOP

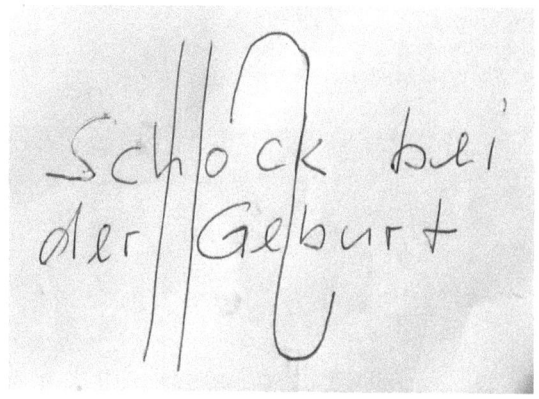

Schlock bei
der Geburt

observers. The neighbor kids saw on a WCP that meant nothing to me, the profile image of a Karl Lagerfeld type. Only then, I realized the picture of hubby. Formerly Peter had tied, in fact, his hair for a while in a ponytail.

After meditation, we see more. For, living in harmony triggers intense feelings. Spiritual energy waves of creation act then amplified. Our mind has by connecting to the cosmic energy, through the law of attraction, a big impact on the world. Thus, we have a responsibility. We are better tapping into the All-knowledge by sitting comfortably, breathing deeply and loosening all muscles. Now we can ask everything. The answers come in the form of thoughts.

What generated the birth trauma?

I laid open to Mr. Braun, what I read in my soul stars. He emailed me then four personal water crystal photo he had photographed in accordance with the method developed by Masaru Emoto. Apparently he hoped that I also come up with an idea.

The Swiss was born two months premature and suffered a birth trauma. Mr. Braun wrote "shock at birth" on a piece of paper and applied it over his handwriting solution symbols. He put a glass with distilled H_2O on it and drank the informed wet. It gave him a good shaking. After several days, he realized that something had left. E. Braun wrapped the paper around a bottle of neutral water. After three days, he photographed the frozen water drops and sent them to me via e-mail with the question: How did you perceive the photos performed by the test with the trauma? Do you see a way of transmitting information?

I looked at the four pictures in sequence and wrote back: *The first crystal reminds me of joyful anticipation/openness, the 2. break in the relationship (with your father?). Above the breakage, I see a broken heart.*

Studying the 3rd photos took a long time. It is also different in the form; something is missing there. There is something mechanical. 4. The calm after the storm. All is well again.

Ernst Braun wrote back then:
Hey, that's very interesting! And ....
It's true. Yikes ...!

51

1. Joyful anticipation/openness

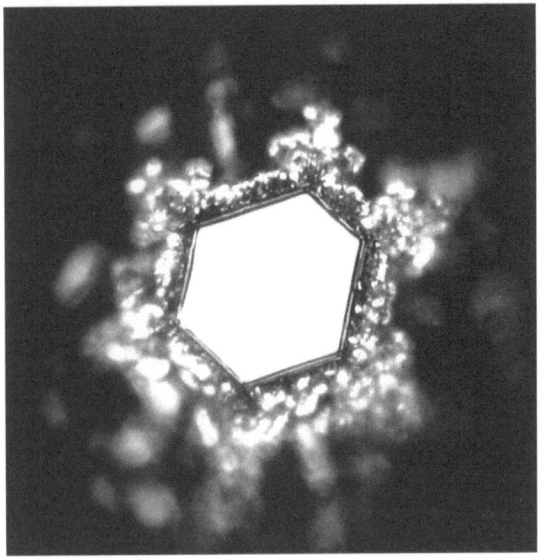

2. Break in the relationship

3. *Something missing, something mechanical*

4. The calm after the storm. All is well again.

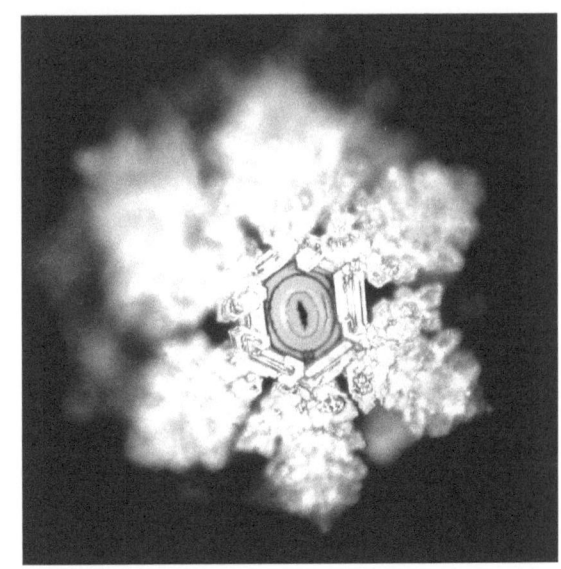

The Swiss artists specialize in photographing soul stars and do this preferably. Nevertheless, E. Braun got the idea that I could interpret some people's soul stars. Immediately the fear of failure touched base with me. But the artist said: We all have these fears. Some stand it, some whitewash it with raspberry sauce or something. Again: Who cares?

I am thinking of an embarrassing experience at the end of a three-month seminar on the development of psychic abilities. A friend had urged me to join.

A man with partly Indian roots and I were the most successful seers. But when the seminar leader Taryn Krivé invited 50 people to let us show off in public, I almost peed my pants. However, the fear is not an issue at home. I may just try it, and you can test my clairvoyant abilities. Prosperous side effect: Painting relaxes deeply and sparks off the eagerness to experiment, imagination and creative crafting.

Living in the cocoon

In this relaxed state, I have found out that the WCP cocoon was a prophecy. I had informed the neutral water with questions for my father who had passed on October 1, 1998. Under my signature, I wrote the question: Dad, do you have something to tell me? I thought of his novel I could not find. He had written it in the early 50s. My brother had read it, but he could not find it.

The interior of the most beautiful water crystal shows the attic. An *eye* looks at a rectangular structure in the far corner. Together with my mother I discovered the shelf there and went stooping to the far corner. Ma said, yes, there he had his writing stuff. I found on the shelf most of his manuscripts.

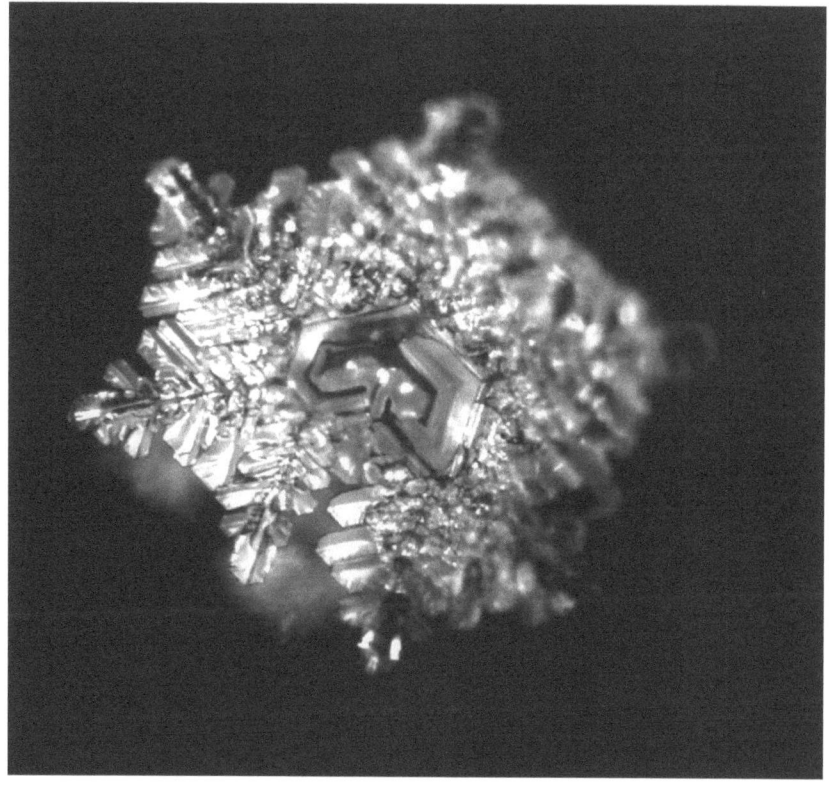

My father's second message was unpleasant, as I found out later. The following two *soul stars* had been clearly predictions.

My mother suffered from Lyme disease, which led to a gradual depression. She felt lonely since she had abandoned her car after an accident with minor car body damage. She missed the freedom to get around, lacked recognition. To have lost her beautiful singing voice broke 's heart. Other reasons for her depression were quarrels and a kind of retirement shock. Alwine Holschuh had given up her last honorary post as an AWO board member. The result of her fifty years of social engagement: an illustrated report in the Echo. Insults, grief and fear seemed to devour her soul slowly.

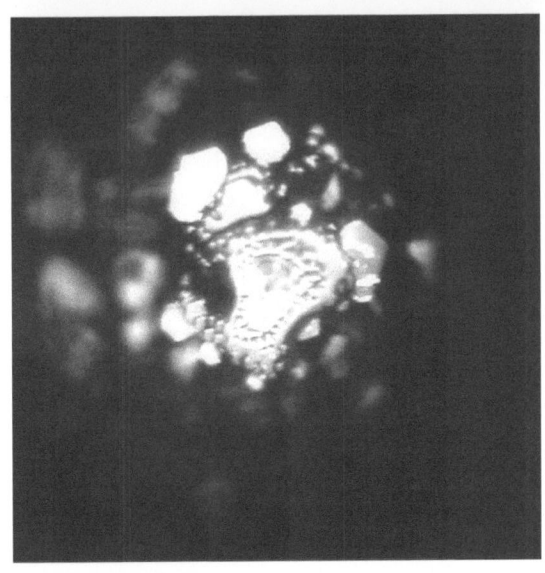

Stone Face and Cocoon

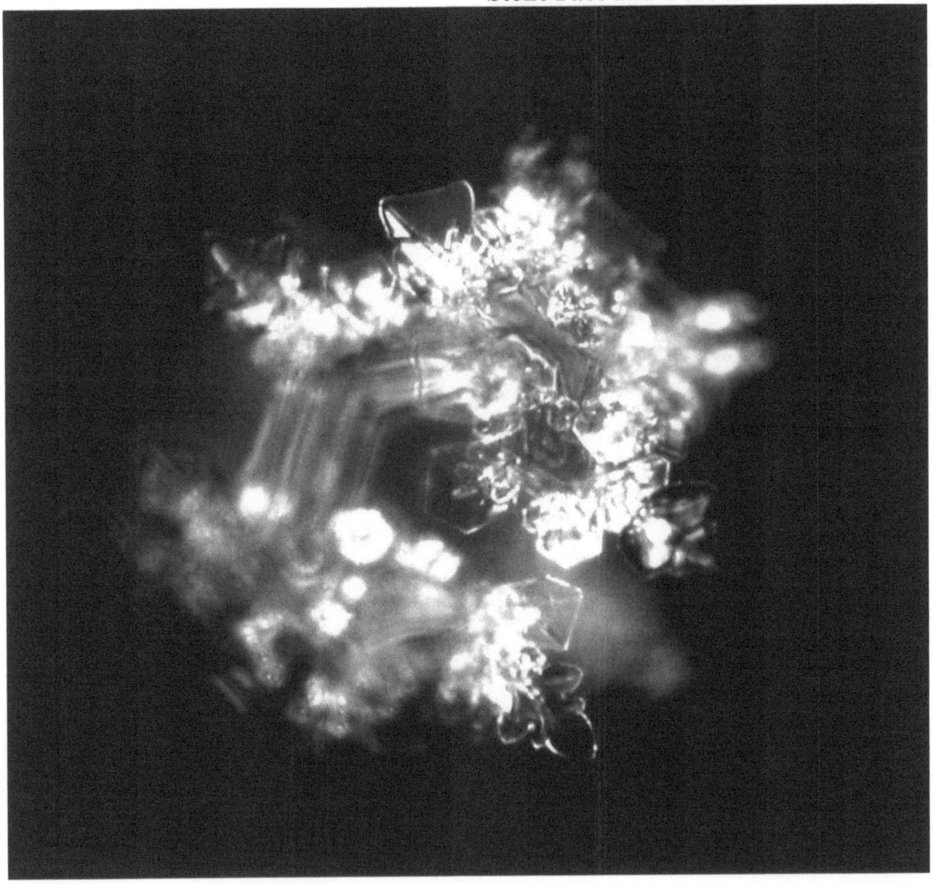

It would be wise to prepare for the retirement by regular meetings of 55-year-old persons with gerontological trained people. With a citizen's income, coupled with ten hours of weekly outreach service, this work could be done voluntarily. Thus, some depression and emotional stupor could be avoided. It would be best to have a school subject in which we could learn constructive relationships by impromptu actions! We would develop tolerance and respect towards all people; partners, parents and children in particular.

Honor at AWO (Worker's Welfare Association)

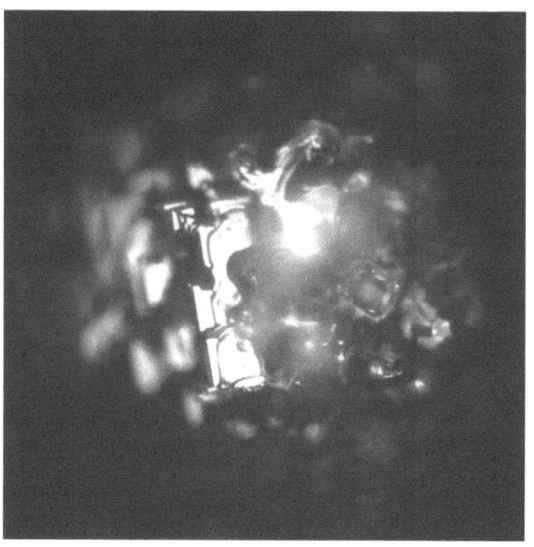

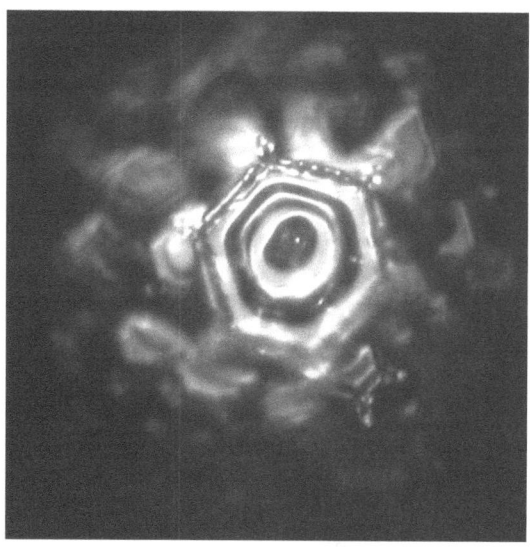

Prepared for the respective periods of life, we might better avoid problems.

The WCP *Stone Face* without crystal formation seems to be the expression of 's loss of her familiar life. For, after an accident, I saw my mother often with a stony face. Speaking of accidents, I found that water crystals with a fragmented structure are related to accidents. The one above shows my husband during a test drive. He broke his shoulder. The WCP on the right is from water informed by a pic of cat Max. He had witnessed the accident of his conspecific Mickey.

The accident Max might have caused by chasing his feline friend was fatal for Micky. The WCP informed by a friend's handwriting shows the same structure, with the point in the middle. His father had died. It so seems that it symbolizes the transition to the other world.

Milestones in my life

E. Braun informed the neutral water with my signature. A few days later, he emailed me 15 water crystal photos. At first I only thought, gosh are they beautiful.

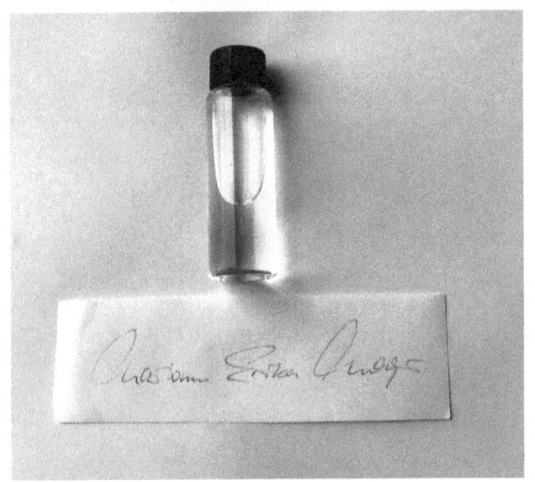

But with each new viewing my *soul stars*, I discovered that most of them reflect my experiences of life!

What is the message of this water miracle? Who is behind this? Because of all personal messages and my supernatural experiences with deceased relatives and acquaintances, it dawned on me, who informed the water: Our DEAD! The essential wet seems to be a medium for the souls. Since they exist on a higher vibrational level, we do not see them, even if they may be around. Apparently my grandmother didn't tell me a fairy story when she said: Your grandpa in heaven always sees what you're doing. I would have less rapidly gotten the idea if I had not read Friedrich Jürgenson's *Voice Transmissions With The Deceased*. In it, the Danish-Swedish artist painter, opera singer and documentary filmmaker explains the contact with the afterlife. He was alerted when listening to taped bird calls by his deceased mother's voice calling his nickname:

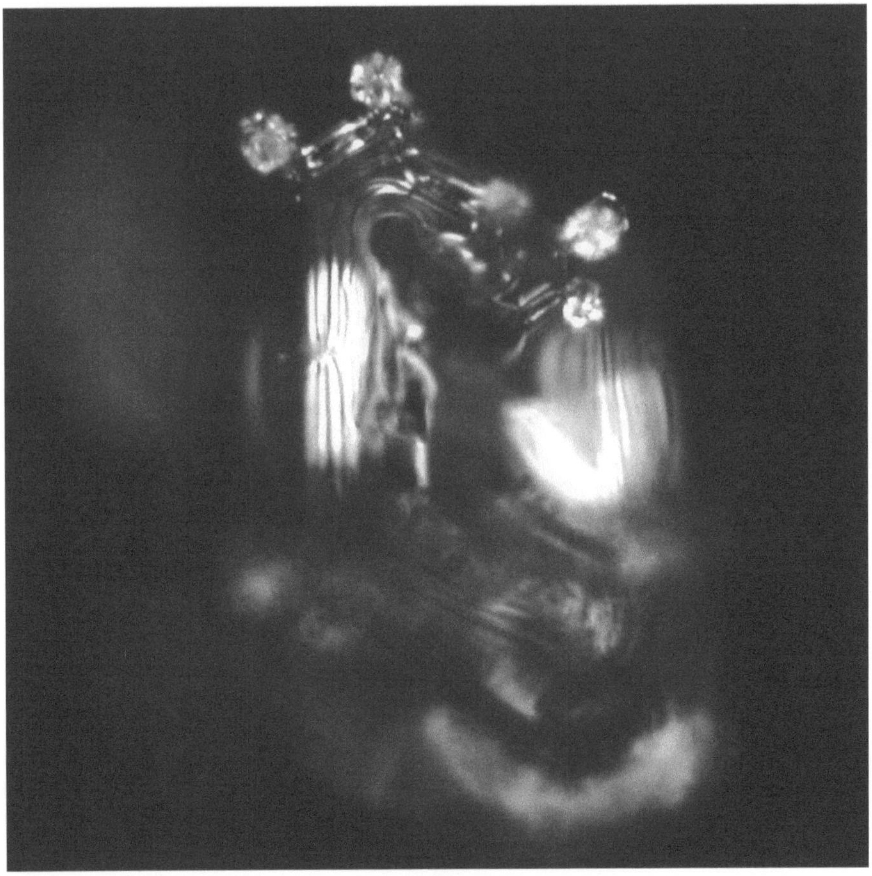

56

Friedel, can you hear me? Here's mommy.

www.vtf.de/schweden.shtml
http://www.tonbandstimmen.de/index.htm

My crystals that reflect pleasant experiences form beautiful shapes. The crises in my life show no distinct forms or dark or parted images.

E. Braun named the water crystal with the praying woman on knees High Priestess. Shortly thereafter, I told my sister-in-law about the water crystal photos and my plans to write a book about it. Renate said: Are you sure you want to do this?

Yes. Why? Are you not concerned you could embarrass yourself? The thing is too important, I can take no account of personal feelings.

Chuckling Renate said: Well, just high priestess.

Had not all searching people who discovered something new been ridiculed?

The WCP with the offset or broken crystal reflects our near-separation. It shows objects from a precarious phase in life with my husband. Peter had for the second time given up smoking and compensated the nicotine withdrawal with vodka. The shape of the crystal's breakage represents Peters silhouette.

Our neighbor friend came in as I studied the crystals on the PC. Looking at the WCP that resembles a picture frame, she said: Is this your wedding photo?

I said: If these water drops are designed of souls, they should know that Peter is much taller. What's that down there? Wow! That's my Moon Hopper. The day I bought it, Peter helped me to get up the ring of the hopping ball. Thus, we are almost equally tall. With

that tool, I had my back muscles strengthened. It stopped the pain while standing for long periods in our gospel choir. Look at that! That's our sign! Yes, definitely Sagittarius. And the eye probably means my childhood *senile* cataract. It looks like the Ohm sign. Perhaps that means: With mineral-poor, high-resistance water, I could have healed the cataract without surgery. Tikale said that And look, the dog has upstanding ears like Sandy. Yes, and the dark one is my unnecessary surgery.

The water informed with our signature or photo shows our characters, the milestones of our lives and our preferences and affairs.

That is also evident in the following report of my former gospel choir friend Dr. Renate Kaiser-Alexnat. By the way, she writes in British English while I write the book in American English.

My many *soul stars* only make sense when the water painters are souls, dead relatives or friends. E. Braun's other clients had only 4 or 8. The many artist painters in my life seem to make the difference. How else could we explain that the Swiss had taken pics of 15 striking water crystals from the H_2O informed by my signature? I am also open to other explanations. Maybe it is as easy as that: The spirit world wants to have this very book.

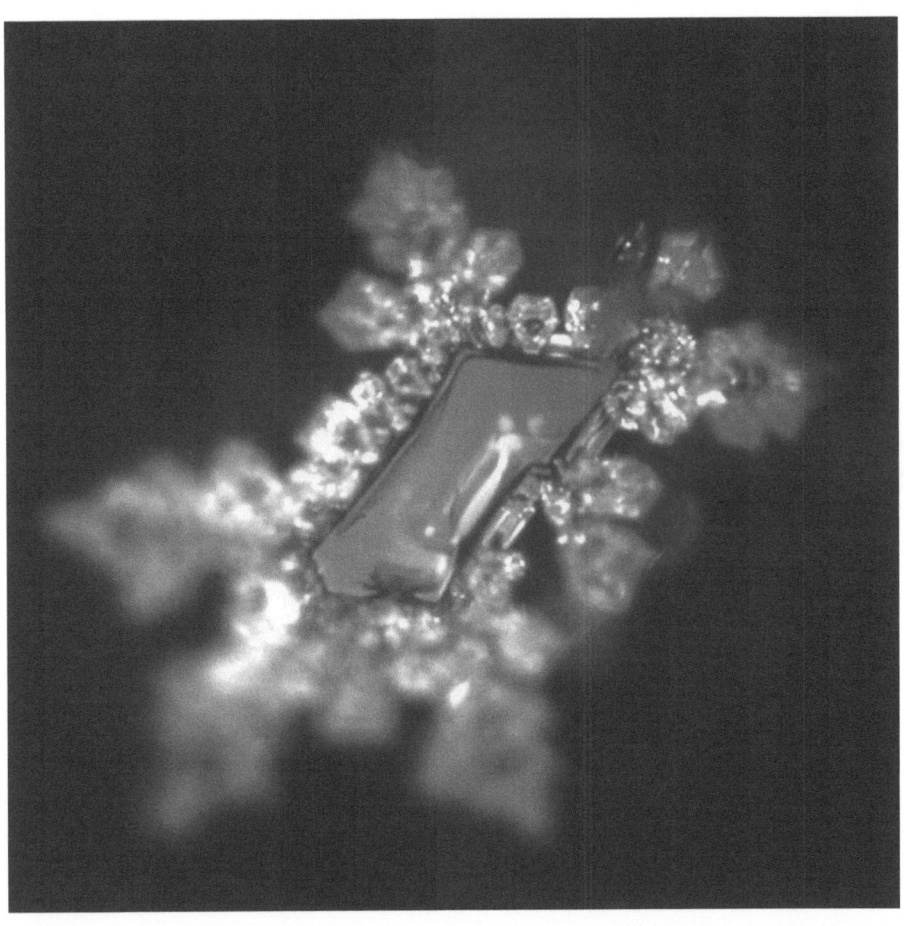

Woad water wonder

From the diary of the agricultural scientist Dr. Renate Kaiser-Alexnat

The number three has always played a significant role in my life. Indeed it even began when I was born as the third of seven children into a farming family. My doctorate was about the resistance of German winter barley cultivars to the Barley Yellow Mosaic Virus. With the aid of classical genetic trisomic analysis and with a set of seven barley strains, each having one of the seven barley chromosomes in triplicate, I was able to localize the resistance gene in question to chromosome 3. Thus the result of my thesis can be summarized with the number three. Later I narrowed down the gene locus with the aid of telotrisomic analysis, in strains of barley, each having one chromosome arm in triplicate, on the long arm of chromosome 3.

The soil borne Barley Yellow Mosaic Virus was first identified in Japan. In Europe it was not confirmed until 50 years later. At that time in Germany cultivars with identical resistance to Barley Yellow Mosaic Virus were still available, even though they were not bred for this particular purpose. Due to the historically earlier appearance of Barley Yellow Mosaic Virus in Japan, the Japanese were well in advance of the Europeans in Barley Yellow Mosaic Virus research. For this reason I visited my Japanese colleagues in connection with an international conference in Kyoto.

After my return from Japan I decided that I would like to go back and the next stay would be longer. As luck would have it, shortly after this my prospective host professor came to Germany. When we met, we arranged my visiting fellowship in the Land of the Rising Sun. Following a selection process by the "Alexander von Humboldt Foundation" I received a grant from the "Japan Society for the Promotion of Science" which made a research stay in Japan financially possible for me. There was as well a strong parallel between my work and that of my host professor. Through his research he had found out that a very important Asian resistance gene against Barley Yellow Mosaic Virus is also located on the long arm of chromosome 3.

My stay in Japan was followed by a three-year research project, in which I was engaged in the cultivation and evaluation of an extensive range of dye producing plant species. Among the dye plants the emphasis of my work was focused on the species dyer's weld which produces a yellow dye. In the human energy system yellow is the colour of the third chakra. After Barley Yellow Mosaic Virus and dye plants, corn pests were the third field of my active research existence.

Because I had been so enthused by the dye plant project, the wish emerged to work with dye plants again. To realise this aspiration within the strictures of the "Institute for Biological Control", where I worked at that time, I did trials testing the inhibitory effect of woad fruit on the germination of other plant seeds as well as the efficacy of woad leaf extracts against some pest and diseases in cultivated plants.

Through the close connection with the woad in my garden, I received information of the metaphysical dimension about this species of plant around Epiphany. Stimulated by the title of the book *"Wunderwesen Wasser"* – "Wonder (being) water" written by my choir friend Dr. Marianne E. Meyer, I created the story book *"Wunderwesen Waid"* – "Wonder (being) woad" to document my most remarkable experiences with this native indigo-bearing plant woad. In the meantime "Woad (being) wonder work", which is how a friend who is specialist in German studies named the book, has been published under the title "Wonder Woad" in English as well.

After Marianne told me enthusiastically about her water crystal photos, I wanted to conduct an experiment of my own. In the week before my birthday in 2008 I set a test-tube with distilled water in the middle of the leaf rosette of my woad plant. On my birthday I sent the woad water sample to the Swiss laboratory of Ernst F. Braun, who specializes in taking photos of water crystals to visualize energetic signatures, using the methods of the Japanese author Dr. Masaru Emoto.

First woad water crystal with triangle

The metaphorical language of water crystals cannot be understood analytically, but instead is perceived intuitively. Marianne explained to me that the first two pictures of a series with water crystals are the most important. When I showed her the pictures of my woad water birthday experiment, Marianne said spontaneously: "In the first picture I see a triangle and the second picture seems to look like a mushroom cloud." I was immediately able to understand her interpretation of the first picture as a triangle, because the three was important to my research work. When I looked at the first

water crystal the European corn borer moth came spontaneously to mind, because at that time I was engaged in the control of corn pests such as this economically destructive moth. The second picture was lost on me.

In the year of the woad water experiment I held my last scientific talk to an international audience at an event involving three conferences. On the way to the conference I landed in England at Birmingham airport early one morning. On the same morning the son of my friend from Tokyo landed together with his friend at the same airport on the outset of their European tour. Our travel preparations were independent of each other and we didn't see each other at the airport. I only accidentally learned about this extraordinary coincidence, because my friend and her husband planned, that the two boys should visit our family at the end of their European trip.

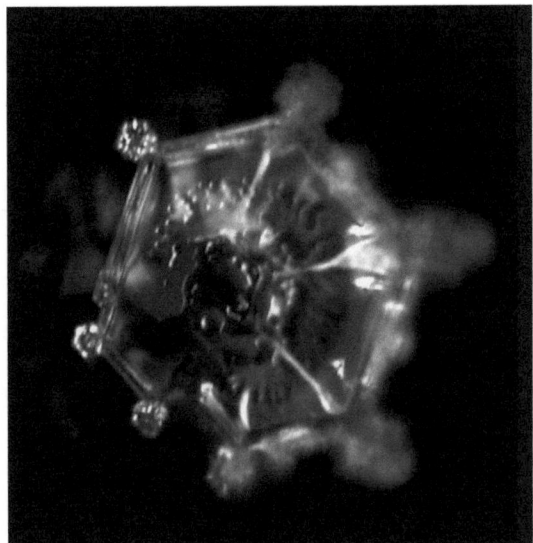

Second woad water crystal with mushroom cloud

Only three years after the woad water experiment, the interpretation by Marianne became clear. The picture of the second water crystal shows something that at that time was a future direction for research. Soon after the earth-quake with its epicentre in Sendai in Japan on 11th March 2011, and the consequent atomic catastrophe of Fukushima, it came to me in a flash that woad is able to draw radioactive substances out of the soil and thus woad cultivation could contribute to the cleaning of the soil. During my occupation with this unexpected theme I found confirmation that in similar manner plants of the family of crucifer, to which woad belongs, are cultivated for the hyper accumulation of heavy metals. However, it was necessary to verify this hypothesis with a scientific experiment.

At first I contacted my friend concerning a woad experiment in Tokyo or Fukushima. The experiment design was comparatively simple, but my friend informed me that such an un-dertaking would most likely come up against closed doors in Japan. However the son of my friend, who visited us at home three years ago, had started a new job in the city of Sendai a few days before the momentous earthquake took place. I hoped that this would provide a chance to make the cultivation experiment happen. Would he personally take a packet of woad seeds that I would send to him, to the agricultural faculty of the Tohoku University? Nevertheless this tactic came to nothing, due to the tense and difficult situation in the troubled area so I temporarily stopped my efforts.

A short time later, an acquaintance called very excitedly and told me that she had visited an event the day before. During the break the conversation turned to Japan. One woman said that that morning she had read in the Stuttgart newspaper that there is a plant, which is used for Prussian blue dyeing, and that it is able to draw radioactive substances from the soil. Im-mediately I contacted the lady and asked her to send me the article *"Mit Preußischblau gegen radioaktives Cäsium"* - "With Prussian blue

against radioactive caesium" printed in the Stuttgart newspaper from the 2nd of April 2011. Although Prussian blue is a natural inorganic pigment and has no bearing on woad, I took this opportunity to spring into action again and send a mail to the Tohoku University in Sendai. But I didn't receive any reply.

One month later, to my great surprise, my Japanese friend sent me a mail with informa-tion about a newspaper article which urged the cultivation of sunflowers around Fukushima. This message from Japan gave me courage for further steps. I contacted the person in the art-icle as well as the Japanese deputy minister for agriculture, because he had assured his sup-port for this proposal. My mail concerning this included a suggestion for a woad cultivation trial in the neighbourhood of Fukushima to verify the above hypothesis with a scientific experiment. I didn't receive a reply to this mail either.

Everything has its time.

"Tree triplets"

On the same day that Marianne informed me, that she had received an acceptance for her third water book, I discovered a formation with three trees standing in a row very close to each other during a walking-tour in the Black Forest. At that time I had not yet read Mari-anne's message. Later on, when I browsed my diary for this essay in Marianne's new water book, I realised that I had begun with this essay exactly five years to the day since my last working day on the active side of research. At the same time a craftsman for whom we had waited a long time, began with the sanding of our parquet floor. In his work I saw a parallel to the theme of cleansing the soil through the cultivation of woad. When reflecting on this coincidence I saw confirmation, that now the time was ripe for the publication of my stories about the woad water wonder.

Last woad water crystal with a Japanese man in the gratitude position

In Japan reverence is expressed by a deep bow. In the last water crystal picture of my birthday trial I see a Japanese man kneeling on the ground in a position of gratitude. This crystal expresses my deep gratitude for the wonderful offer of assistance.

If one considers scientific development, it is clear that the crossover between spiritual and material becomes more and more verifiable. At the interface between a pure materialistically orientated research and a holistic contemplation, the view

turns from the pure material to the spirit, which quasi represents the motor for the embodiment of the material. The water crystal pictures confer a visible expression to this universal knowledge.

In the awareness of the entity of nature and the metaphysical around us, I see the key to a true science, in which the separation between the humanities and the natural sciences will disappear with increasing awareness.

In a particular phase of life I realized: "Everything is absolutely logical, each stone - how it sits, each blade of grass - how it stands." My previous perspective of the world extended, whereby I watched the game of life from a higher perspective. For years I wrote down my experiences to publish them in a book called "Researches of a soul". Meanwhile I accepted that life is a mystery that only God can comprehend.

Michelstadt, 19th December 2014

Renate Kaiser-Alexnat

Institute for Dye Plants www.dyeplants.de Human and Plant www.menschundpflanze.de

Supplementary notes

Before I finished the German version of this essay on 21st December 2013, I gave the woad water essay to a colleague with a request for feedback. When I asked him for his opinion, he showed me a document on which he was currently working at that time. As though by accident he pointed to a passage, in which the date 11th March 2013 was readable. Immediately I remembered that it was the anniversary of the earthquake in Sendai. My translation of the essay into the English version was finished exactly one year later to the day of my request for feedback from my colleague.

IV. WATER AND HEALTH

The sun doctor Auguste Rollier, head of the famous Swiss Rollier Sanatorium gave his patients only rainwater and water from melted snow to drink because it not as hard as normal water. Many indigenous people drank for centuries mineral-free glacier and rainwater and enjoyed good health. Today, in most environs, the rain water is too heavily burdened. One way, to demineralize ordinary water is a steam distillation. Dr. Rollier strengthened his patient's body's defense by revitalizing sun baths in the mountain air and body activities to toughen up. The moral and spiritual well-being had been ensured by patient's choirs, libraries, Boy Scouts, summer schools and a clinic manufacture. Here, the sick could pursue a manual activity.

Paul C. Bragg, the father of the health movement in America, had been abandoned as a teenager by US doctors. He cured his tuberculosis in Dr. Rollier's clinic and shared his health rules with his countrymen: Pure water, good food, fresh air and the sunshine, breathing techniques and exercises.

Hard water he holds responsible for the development of atherosclerosis and gall bladder, kidney and bladder stones. Bragg discovered that in areas where drinking water is very hard, people calcified earlier and stronger. To descale, he recommends a one-week fasting with steam distilled water and a little lemon juice, possibly with some honey.

Only bathe in the mineral water, but never drink it because inorganic minerals accumulate in joints and arteries. The blood vessels in the brain ossify like a limestone cave.

Light, air, water, sun, relaxation & exercise

I have explained this type of treatment in my self-help book. It is based on seven healing vitality rules to maintain a proper functioning immune system under the following headings. I will bring it out in English, end of 2015.

1. Clean air and the sun are vital to us.
2. Natural food tastes better and is doing well.
3. Regular exercise is effective against diseases of civilization.
4. Pure water can be more than brushing your teeth.
5. Getting enough sleep, resting and relaxing exercises are gentle healer of nature.
6. Joyful working in our dream job makes us happy.
7. Turning to the soul and spirit fulfills our life.

Our biological needs are not different from the ones of our ancestors. But today, the air is not as fresh, the water, not as pure and the food not as nutritious anymore. Regular exercise is missing, too. The rest period in front of the telly doesn't seem to be the right one either. And, how about joy in your work and meditation?

With an emphasis on regularity, all these seven directives today are just as essential for a healthy and joyous life.

Is the sun actually harmful?

Yes and no. Paracelsus said: Dosis sola venenum facit. Only the dose makes the poison. A US study contradicts the theory that UV rays are responsible for the skin cancer epidemic. From 1974 to 1985 the amount of UV radiation was measured in the US, reaching the surface of the earth. The sunburn-causing radiation frequency should be determined. The number of skin cancers in the United States doubled within this period of 11 years. Since, the part of the ultraviolet light fell by 0.7%, this contradicts the theory that UV light is the reason for the skin cancer epidemic. The UV rays of sunlight stimulate the thyroid and increase hormone production.

Thus, they speed up the metabolism. This helps in weight loss and improves muscle development. www.ener- chi.com/enerchiwp/wp-content/uploads/2011/11/Heile-dich.pdf

When animals are kept indoors, they shall also fatten faster. In Portugal, chickens seem to have an outlet because they have only a fraction of the fat of an ordinary German chicken. We also gain weight when we sit most of the time at home on the couch and avoid the sun. Slowly we get to the truth, that a lack of sunlight is one of the biggest risk factors for diseases.

To demineralize and release of toxins or acidic crystals, Bragg recommends a one-week fasting with distilled water, a little fresh lemon juice and ¼ to ½ teaspoon of honey if desired. He also advises taking in lots of fruits, vegetables, and fresh fruit juices.

Detuned body fluid as a cause of disease

In English, humor means humor, mood, spirits and body fluid. Ill-humor means anxious, sullen, grumpy, sore, acidic, sourly.

How can we tune the 40 to 60 liters of water that we carry around so that there is no sick sour-puss? One thing is to improve the poor quality of our drinking water. We can also activate our right brain and thus increase our vibration frequency via dynamic meditation, positive imagination and wholesome food and livings. Let's try positive thinking. We can apply Émile Coué's mantra-like conscious autosuggestion: "Every day, in every way, I am getting better and better." José Silva also empowers us with his method of positive affirmations. I like this one: *Positive thoughts attract everything I wish magnetically towards me.*

The water in our cells serves as a memory storage. Depending on the nature of our memories, we react in a good mood or out of tune. Negative emotional influence or physical stress can cause blockages in the energy fields and eventually disease.

How can we set the distorted self-resonant damaged cells back to their ideal natural frequency? We begin best by using our free will in such a way that we avoid thoughts, feelings and words that express imperfection. This allows dissonant vibrations to override.

The lack of good water is a major cause of the increase of diseases in addition to the lack of rest and contemplation. For, as already mentioned, H_2O is only an elixir of life if it is not violated within pipelines. The natural movement of the water is largely destroyed by the pressure ratio in the pipe. It thus loses its geometric structure, ergo its information content and its vitality.

Confined and tortured, H_2O comes about only as a depressive muck. Such water is not able to solve slags moreover, flood them from the body.

This is the reason for the increasing poisoning and disharmony of our body water. We observe the free-flowing water in nature, we can see that it moves curving. Look at the next riding in the rain as it moves down the windshield of your car in meanders. Water is not subject to gravity, so it does not run directly down but moves ovately in wavy lines. For this reason, river regulation affects catastrophic; e. g., the cooling effect of vegetation curves ceases to exist. This leads to flooding. Also, the gas exchange with the atmosphere and the inclusion of cosmic energies. Thus, the vitality and regenerative capacity of the water suffers.

We tend to feel more brilliant than nature. Sin floods and fires are evidence of our mistakes. However, our primal fear of floods, droughts and forest fires fueled by the climate change should not paralyze us. It should make us learn from our mistakes and from nature.

Except for our citizen's initiative we may

not have any influence on the temperature of the river water. However, we can do something for our body water. We can stop to inventing ever more sophisticated methods to push us from physical exertion. As a result, our body fluids thicken and thus provide a breeding ground for disease.

If we move too little, our body water feels as violated as the tap water!

On the other hand, it reacts very pleasantly when we revive it by dancing or jumping on a trampoline. Dr. Samuel West recommends bouncing on the trampoline for activating the lymph and for discharging the waste products. With inline skating, I like to move in wavy lines.

Complex body with simple operation

If we want to stay happy and healthy, it is necessary that we follow the basic laws of nature! Diseases originate in the shade of unhappy thoughts. They are primarily the result of a conflict between soul and spirit, or the likes or the willing part of the soul. Thus, they can be cured only by spiritual effort. By harmonious tones, loving words, and positive thoughts we can structure our body water and heal ourselves. This will also be necessary when with the growing number of diseases the conventional medicine is at her wit's end, leading in the direction of an economic fiasco.

What are the factors that affect our well-being? On the physical level, we do not drink enough pure water, eat too much, too fat, too sweet or too one-sided. We are moving far too little, too many toxins accumulate in the body, we live too hectic and miss out on the real things in life. Mentally, the Western world suffers from the extensive exclusion from the metaphysical thinking. As compensation for the true values of life, such as love,

humility, faith, hope, equality and nonviolence serve worldly wealth, desire, pleasure, and ambition.

It is mainly about to fulfill our tasks with joy at heart and to follow the dictates of our soul.

If we listen again to that inner voice of conscience and are guided by our soul, we will fix our shortcomings gradually so that health and happiness are gainable.

In medical education, the treatment of symptoms is in the foreground. If the head hurts, it gets scanned. The pain is numbed with chemical drugs. Because the cause of suffering is not addressed, given time toxins accumulate in the body. Mostly suffering is just the reaction of not having had enough rest or fresh air, or the spine may have been overloaded. In the latter case, usually extensive stretching exercises are sufficient to achieve freedom from symptoms.

On the spiritual level, there are feelings of fear, guilt, doubt, depression or irritability, which disturb our peace of mind and express a lack of love.

We better drink only water without dissolved CO_2, otherwise the organism has a tremendous work to excrete the acid or its salts (carbonates). If we do not drink it about ½ to 1 hour before eating solid food, the body takes the necessary water from the cells and therefore dries out. In the course of the years, this leads to a number of diseases based on lack of water and the associated storage of various poisons.

Instead nibbling chips, biscuits or sausage, we better chose carrots or green papaya strips with avocado dip. It is all a matter of habit. Veggie snacks are not metabolized acid-forming and do not dry out. We will feel well and have regular bowel movements. The properly flushed kidneys produce clear, well-smelling urine. Thus, the poisoning of the excretory organs is prevented. Daily 1½ to 2 liters of pure water, at least half an hour before eating ensures that acid crystals to dissolve from the deposits in the joints. Thus, we do not have to suffer from inflammation. A bowl of soup or water-rich fruits, salad and vegetables also have a purging effect. See Chapter Arthritis - proper purging helps fight joint pain.

Since each individual metabolizes differently, we better observe our body, how it reacts to certain behavior and eating habits. For simplicity, we can use a questionnaire as in my Psyllium book. It includes a multi-page food list that also shows the glycemic index, calorie content and acidic or alkaline-forming effect of the food. As we search ourselves, we create more knowledge than by memorizing the entire clinical dictionary with its terrible excesses of human errors. However, we may have to atone for the sins of our ancestors. They may have abused drugs, nicotine, and alcohol or wastefully consumed pesticides and industrial chemicals. Strolling as walking cesspools through life, they may have charged the offspring with genetic defects. Yet, even then we can be happy and healthy if we behave naturally. Especially when taking full baths in activated water. Over time, we can even reduce hereditary damages.

* We learn from our experience because each organism reacts differently. Let's explore it according to the principle of cause and effect.

* If our body reacts with symptoms, we ask better ourselves: How could we have violated the laws of nature?

* Our bodies need living water, fresh air, rest, and exercise.

* We need not be afraid but have to realize that we have it in our hands to be healthy or sick.

* Clear urine and daily bowel movements

indicate well-being.

* Noodles, rice and pastries such as bread, pizza and pasta need much water to digest.

The following two chapters cover the internal and external irrigation.

The cleaning power of water-rich food

Water transports nutrients to the cells. It absorbs waste and discharge it from the body. Just as we clean ourselves externally, we better provide for the internal cleanliness, otherwise the dirt deposits and causes problems. We would stink if our skin had no contact with water for weeks. Similarly, if we would not drink water or eat fruit, salad and vegetables we'd need a gas mask passing through our bodies.

Solid food does not clean. For cleaning the window, we too need water and no sausage or cheese.

Therefore, water-containing food is essential. The best solution to discharge toxins is the water in naturally grown fruits and vegetables. However, we eat sprayed fruits which cause acidity. The cleansing effect of organically grown products we could experience on our month-long journey through Morocco. Chickens are often offered alive and dangle over the open counter. Fly-strewn mutton pieces do not stimulate the appetite either. Therefore, many campers are limited to the consumption of fruits, vegetables, rice, legumes, and fish. Most fruits and vegetables in North Africa cost 25-50 cents per kg. These prices do not allow expensive fertilizers and pesticides. Formerly, we have also done well without them.

If we don't feel comfortable when water fasting we may take more water-rich foods. I enclose a fruit day once a week and perform every two to three months the purification process of the Seneca Indians recommended by Hanna Kroeger. That suppose to prevent atherosclerosis. We eat on day one only hydrous fruit. On the second day, there are only herbal teas sweetened with a little honey. On the 3rd day, we eat only vegetables, raw or steamed. On the 4th day, we have a freshly made vegetable broth. This diet plan cleanses on the first day the colon, our inner garbage dump. On the 2nd day, we discharge all toxins, excess salts, and calcium deposits from muscles, tissues and organs. On the 3rd day, we feed the gut with a mineral-rich diet and on the 4th we mineralize the blood, lymph, and internal organs. Already after a short time a detox and improved oxygenation of the blood is achieved. We best combine it with exercise in the fresh air and perform Kneipp's water treatments or lymphatic cleansing baths as in the following section.

* Artificial sweeteners bring humans, animals and plants in a chemical deregulation and lead to addiction.

* Clean water and water-containing foods cleanse and purify.

* Disease has to do with the poisoning of the body. The only sensible therapy is the excretion of toxins with pure water.

* A fruit day per week rids the body of impurities. It prevents premature aging and gives beautiful skin and hair.

Purification of the lymphatic system by taking mineral baths

If we eat suboptimally, the lymph can accumulate in the abdomen due to intestinal inflammation or other enteric problems. Such an overload of the to a nutritional disorder of the spine. The lack of supply of the spinal nerves results in pain. The head of the

Schlosspark Klinik in Gersfeld/Rhön recommends a Mayr cure (dry rolls and milk) and specific abdominal massages (2008).

We can also activate the lymphatic system regularly so that it can transport dead cells and toxins from all organs and body parts. This cleansing and healing of the body can be done by full baths in a good water such as via turbulence activated H_2O. We could also swim in the mineral-rich waters, such as the Dead Sea.

*When bathing, a basic cleaning
and lymph relief of the body takes place.
With that a genetic load can be reduced.*

For a mineral bath, we can add the salt of the Dead Sea or the mineral-rich herbs such as nettles or horsetail to the bath water.

Before and after a half bath time, we rub the body (always stroke towards the heart!) with a sisal glove, dry brush or rough sponge.

This opens the pores and washes out the toxins. Before and during bathing, drinking plenty of water or herbal tea reinforces the removal of radiation and toxins. Loosening acid crystals can cause pain in the head or the fingers and toes. That will disappear quickly when we drink alkaline water. Also, Spirulina, the juice of half a lemon, half a teaspoon of bicarbonate of soda or other natural antacids dissolved in water help to relieve pain.

Vigorous stretching, especially stretching after bathing leads to a pleasant feeling of warmth in the back.

The *Five Tibetan Rites are* a system of ancient exercises that are best suited to regenerate the spinal column. The first rite of the Tibetan rituals, formulated by Peter Kelder, is simple: 21 right turns with outstretched arms. That ensures the natural movement of our body water and invigorates the energy centers (chakras) and glands. Through the four other rites that stretch the spine, all the organs are better supplied with blood, oxygen, and nutrients.

Deep breathing, jumping on soft ground or the trampoline and brush massages also stimulate the lymph.

Problems with the lymphatic circulation are often associated with water retention of the feet and hands. They respond well to the application of cold water and massage. Circling the arms and the *lymph cradle* also relieve the lymphatic system. We place ourselves on the abdomen, forming fists and push them onto the right and left groin. By moving the hips back and forth, we massage the lymph nodes. With swollen lymph glands in the neck, a poultice with cold rosemary tea soothes the pain.

* Mineral baths regenerate the lymphatic system and the entire body.

* Cold water and massage help lymphatic congestion (swollen hands, feet, eyes).

* The *5 Tibetans* stimulate the glands and detoxify the body.

What influences our body water?

We are daily exposed to electromagnetic fields via electromagnetic pollution from computers, televisions, clock radios, and other devices. Our body water is thereby electrically charged, thickened and acidified. Other sources of charging are X-ray and microwave radiation, drugs, cigarettes, cosmetics, dyes, preservatives, spirals, birth control pills, and other medicines. Each injection changes the frequency spectrum of the vaccinees, therefore, the number of vibrations in a unit cell. This can lead to acute reactions, temporary impairments or after-effects.

Irradiated or dead food from cooking can change or delete the cell vibration. For instance, in the milk, the calcium bound to the milk protein casein shows under the microscope as a matted mass. According to the professors Werner Kollath and Lothar Wendt that occurs already in short-term heating (pasteurization). The liver cannot utilize this matted mass. The consumption leads to slagging of the arteries and protein storage diseases. So for the body receives no usable calcium, it takes it from the bones. Therefore, the osteoporosis in countries with high dairy consumption is particularly widespread.

How harmful heated milk is, shows the Oxford study. A calf that drank the pasteurized milk of his mother and died after a few weeks. Another English examination revealed: Cats that eat only food and water out of the microwave, die within a month!

Already in 1995, Lai and Singh detected degenerative changes of acute exposure to low-intensity microwaves in rat brain cells (increased DNA single-strand breaks).

As mentioned, Masaru Emoto showed that the waves of certain thoughts, words and musical works are affecting the water. Our body consists about 70% of the versatile element. Depending on the influences, the water reacts positive or negative. A friendly tone, uplifting music, and soothing words were shown to create harmonious and beautiful water crystals. Such structured body water removes toxins and provides for our physical and mental well-being. In contrast, insults or heavy metal music with horrible texts leads to disharmony, thus to destroy water crystals, and consequently forms deposits.

Microwave foods, pasteurized or UHT milk and discordant music are causing more and more young people suffer from arteriosclerosis. Even little children can endure strokes.

So let us better not destroy the harmony of our body water and the beautiful water crystals with heavy metal music and insults. That is why regular meditation is good for revitalizing our body water.

Besides uplifting music, Tai Chi, Yoga, mineral baths and meditation I presented in *Wunderwesen Wasser* a particularly effective way of strengthening the water dynamics in the body. In the 70's and 80's, under the leadership of Johann Tikale, I was involved in exploring the relationships and dependencies of the health of the people of geological and hydrological conditions. On the internet, I found a document by Norbert Harthun, which also deals with the work of the Forschungskreis für Geo-Hydro-Biologie in Igelsbach/Neckar.

home.arcor.de/gdn3/Seiten/Publikationen/Wa sserTranszendenz.doc

By the suggestion of Dr. Walter Notteboom, Tikale developed a system in which the healing of the so-called diseases of civilization was performed by cleansing the lymph and regenerating the spine. According to Tikale, the organism must detoxify via the lymphatic system. The blockages thus, the in the spine manifesting trauma of the body are to be dissolved.

I joined the former research circle almost 40 years ago. The native Bohemian told me, if I would have come earlier, my surgery (cataract in both eyes) would not have been necessary. My mother was lucky. An orthopedist told her that the stiffening of her spine was irreversible. She was not able to move her vacuum cleaner or hold her baby grandson. After she had laid down, it took her a while to painfully get up again. However, after three month of lymphatic cleansing she was flexible again until old age. With revitalized water, deacidification, lymphatic cleansing, we can regenerate all tissues in the body, even clouded lenses.

Only recently, I was able to experience that Astaxanthin would have been another way to prevent cataract. The microalgae Haematococcus pluvialis produces this beta-carotenoid. This antioxidant is a hundred times stronger than other radical scavengers. Bob Capelli sent me his book on Astaxanthin. When I flew to USA 3½ years ago, I bought six bottles of Astaxanthin for experimentation. I took the capsules on a regular basis. Some 18 months later, I thought my right eye had deteriorated. I blamed the permanent work on the PC. However, examining my eyes, there was a surprise: The right eye needed a weaker lens by almost four diopters! The left eye improved by 1½ diopters. For many years, I take Spirulina. However, Astaxanthin seems to be a much more potent antioxidant and healer.

* Electrosmog charges, thicken and acidifies our body water.

* Microwave food, drugs, and vaccines change or delete the cell vibration.

* Soft music and uplifting words create beautiful water crystals.

* Johann Tikale developed a method, to bring water molecules charged by negative influences back to their natural ground state.

* The removal of disturbances brings about the healing of degenerative diseases via lymph cleansing and spine regeneration.

* The regeneration of the cells and the conversion of cell water can also be done by modern water activation technique.

The body's cries for the lively elixir

Without water, there is no salvation

J. -W. v. Goethe

The poetic genius was also a naturalist. Whether colors, trees, stones, Goethe studied nature like no other. And he took baths like no other. His records testify how crucial the spa therapy was to him. Good things do come to those who wait. We best wait in the bath.

Depending on the age and health of the human body, it contains 55 to 80% water. In order to prevent disease, the water balance must be maintained. One glass of water, 30 minutes before each meal helps digestion. Two glasses of water in the morning helps the internal organs, stimulates the metabolism and detoxifies the body. Water transports essential nutrients to our cells. It also discharges unfavorable substances through the various channels of elimination such as the intestine, ureter, and skin. Less well known:

One glass of water before bathing reduces blood pressure. Also, a glass of water before going to bed prevents convulsions, heart attacks and strokes.

We drink, therefore, better daily 1½ - 3 liters (per kg 30 ml) of pure, living water as often as possible and take a full bath. With water deficiency diseases, the metabolism suffers an imbalance consistently, as the lack of liquid leads to malfunctions. In epilepsy, Parkinson's and Alzheimer's, the cerebral metabolism is disturbed due to insufficient water reaching the brain. But especially in the brain and nervous system, the body water in a healthy organism is very organized. It is, therefore, also referred to as liquid crystal. Many of you might say, if it were that easy, why don't we know about these things. Conventional medicine recognizes, too that the body needs to be fed liquids, but most doctors advise their patients only to drink a lot. That it should be pure water without gas and chemical flavors, is little known. Even in hospitals, patients are offered sparkling water: But water with dissolved CO_2 thus, carbon dioxide, does not belong to the body.

In our fast-moving world, environmental conditions and habits are constantly changing. What's in today's out tomorrow. Formerly, many diseases were not existent because the groundwater was not contaminated with pesticides and heavy metals.

* Fizz, designer water, coffee, tea, cola, soda, beer and wine will dry out the body.

* With epilepsy, Parkinson's and Alzheimer's the brain and nervous system are missing pure structured water.

How much water does a person need?

Our body contains about two-thirds of water, the brain even 90%. In the course of life, the water content decreases in the body. Infants consist of about 80% of the body mass, very old people usually of less than 60%. To compensate for the daily water loss through perspiration, respiration, urine, alcohol, coffee etc., we need depending on body weight 1½ to 3 liters of water.

As a rule of thumb, 30 ml of water per kg body weight

With 50 kg usually 1½ l suffices, with 65 kg, we need 2 l, with 100 kg 3 l. On hot summer days, with fever, diarrhea or vomiting we need twice or three times as much.

If we do not drink enough water and eat water-poor foods, such as bread, pastries, pasta and pizza, a rationalization mechanism sets in for maintaining bodily functions. It occurs an internal release of histamine to keep the water reserves (see chapter asthma/allergy). The brain, which is only a fiftieth of the body weight but contains 20% of the circulating blood, has the absolute priority.

With all brain diseases, water is the optimal solution that makes us not only healthier but also conscious!

Charged with healing information and life energy, water gives the body the power to heal itself and regenerate.

Going easy on a low flame, we don't feel the dehydration immediately. Only when the body sends signals of distress, such as thirst, dry mouth or loss of appetite, we recognize the need to drink. But the lack of water can cause some discomfort trouble when no thirst is felt.

* Especially in brain diseases applies: Drink more water or eat water-containing fruits, such as melons and oranges.

* We better don't wait for the thirst signals.

* With exercise, fever, diarrhea, vomiting or in summer we need much more water.

Physical signs of lack of water

If we feel powerless and often exhausted or are afflicted with headaches or nausea, that can be the first signs of dehydration. Chronic constipation and highly colored, caustic urine are already pronounced symptoms of a lack of water. Particularly far advanced is the dehydration when the face looks like it is covered with a thin parchment paper that is stretched to the breaking point. The eyes look tired from small wrinkly slits. In any case, we urgently need the vivid blue gold. Only structured water can solve and wash out pollutants. H_2O is considered dead if it does not form molecule clusters.

Clusters enclose germs and toxins and transport them from the body.

Tap water, unless it is activated by water energizing technique, is generally dead. See Part II.

A disturbed water balance can endanger our health significantly since the essential solvent is urgently needed to detoxify our body. Constipation causes toxins not to be eliminated. The blood thickens. The lack of excretion of harmful substances usually leads to renal failure. It can form kidney stones and urinary tract inflammations.

* Headache is a precursor of dehydration.

* If the stool is too hard and the urine dark and stinks awful, H_2O is missing.

* Wrinkled parchment skin is the most obvious sign of lack of water.

* Water deficiency leads to constipation, toxins remain in the body, the blood becomes thick, kidney problems may arise.

Strengthening the water balance in the body

If we consider the body to be the temple of our soul and treat it with care and respect, it will serve us well. We strengthen the water element by drinking plenty of pure water and eat water-containing fruits and vegetables. With additional affirmative thoughts and words, we generate interferences with our body water. Emoto showed that with such mutual influences distorted crystals return to their beautiful shape. In his view, that also happens just by looking at the water crystal photos.

If we consume too little water-containing foods, we can balance this shortcoming with special herbs. Among them are licorice, ginseng, and comfrey. We best take them in conjunction with hot water, vegetable soup or fresh fruit juices. In general, the water element enhances by sweet, salty and sweet and sour dishes.

Is the tissue already severely dehydrated, we best eat a miso soup.

Miso is a pulp of rice and soy, fermented in addition of mushrooms. It is useful against radioactive contamination. In his cancer book, the macrobiotics guru Michio Kushi,

---

The following symptoms of dehydration are to be observed:

With a water loss of

up to 3%:	dry mouth, thirst, decreasing urine production
4 to 6%:	fatigue, weakness, nausea, motor disorders, rapid heartbeat, elevated temperature
7 to 11%:	dizziness, headache, shortness of breath, blood deficiency, inability to walk
over 11%:	confusion, convulsions, delirium
over 20%:	death

(Medicom, 14/2000)

relates to the head of the hospital. That was near the dropping of the Nagasaki bomb. He gave the personnel every day a miso soup. None of his staff had been haunted by the otherwise severe radiation damage.

But we better do not rush with the re-flotation of the tissue with miso soup. Because of the long dehydration, the kidneys may be damaged. We know that a dried sponge soaks up all the water immediately. When we drink too much at once, the kidneys cannot filter the excess water, and it can get into the lungs. So we drink only one glass of water, in addition, a few days later one more. We better measure how much water we have drunk and urine produced. If we pass enough water, we can drink more.

According to Hildegard of Bingen, we increase the healthy fluids by a certain diet such as cooked beets, cooked celery and raw masor cooked fennel. With a diseased intestine or for the deacidification it is recommended to drink beans water: Soak a cup of beans overnight with plenty of water, remove the water completely, cook beans in a pot full of fresh water 1½ hours, add some oil or butter and crystal salt, drink one cup of the warm broth slowly and keep the rest in the fridge. Drinking 1 to 2 cups of the bean water and 2 liters of boiled water throughout the day, stimulates the body osmosis.

We regulate our water balance by sitting on a lake, river or waterfall. We could also walk through wet grass or snow or wading in the mud and singing in the rain. I have even tried to make the rain, but not with Wilhelm Reich's Cloud Buster rain machine. My cosmic Orgone technology related to requests via mantras, pictures, and a specially composed rain song. Was it beginners luck that it rained three days later, after months of drought?

Also partial or full baths, Kneipp therapy,

steam treatments, water aerobics and massages, as well as all sports, in cool water strengthen the water balance. Mothers can give birth to their children by water delivery.

Let us in many ways turning to the water!

We can buy a splashing fountain or adorn ourselves with beautiful gems of the water. They include moonstone, topaz, yellow sapphire and rock crystal. Also, there is a the sound of the moon corresponding mantra of water: It is Som, spoken SOUM. According to the traditional Indian medicine (Ayurveda), this mantra strengthens the internal stability. It relieves stress and helps with a sense of natural tension. It fuels the nerves and the subtle energy channels. It ensures a relaxing sleep and leaves the mind to calm and mature (Edde, 1992).

* Sweet, sour and sweet and sour dishes strengthen the water element.

* If we are very dehydrated, water consumption should be gradually increased.

* The water balance is strengthened when we drink structured water, eat plenty of water-containing organic fruits, perform Kneipp's water therapy or come otherwise in contact with H_2O.

Anxiety causes dry mouth and vice versa

Who does not know the phenomenon of a tongue sticking on the palate when we are anxious and excited? From that, we can conclude: Those who are often afraid and are depressed by anxiety, frustration, worry and petty suffering, need not be surprised if the body dries out. If we constantly fear something terrible could happen, the organism is under so much pressure that a natural balance in the body can be barely maintained.

Fear, hatred and evil have nothing to do

with our nature. Our true nature is based on trust and love! Therefore, instead of saying, of course, I was scared, we use daily positive affirmations. We best practice the loving contact with one another and all living things. Being gentle with ourselves is most important, for love drives away fear, guilt, grief and anger. But sometimes the fear creeps in our brooding chamber like a sneaky gremlin, sits heavy on the chest, constricts us by the throat and takes our breath away. The musings are not always our invention. Often we pick up negative thoughts of anxious people. So better immediately return the doom and gloom back to the sender!

An impressive example of sending fear yielded a friend: Her adventurous ex-husband had traveled alone in the South American jungle. A few days after his departure, she heard the news of three hostages, but without worrying because she was in complete confidence on his luck. One morning, however, she was startled by most horrifying pictures. She wished to dispel them immediately. But, time and again, the demons crept in. It got so bad that she was out of breath when climbing stairs and suffered from palpitations. At noon, her ex-father-in-law called anxiously inquiring whether she had received a postcard. She knew straight off what caused her restlessness. It was a thought transference.

We better pay attention to our thoughts
and banish all negative ones,
because they harm us and our loved ones!

That illustrates our attachment to and dependence on others. The thoughts of the beggar can harm the millionaire. Therefore, it is essential that all are doing well. A redistribution benefits us all!

Perhaps it would be better to switch channels on negative news programs. Why should we burden ourselves with the daily horror stories? By enduring the constant litany of crimes and violence, we help to spread the horror with which evil will remain in the world. By the way, we may have less violent movies in the future. Brad Bushman and Angelica Bonacci from Iowa State University in Ames studied TV viewer behavior. They found out that when watching a TV show with violent or perverse sexual content the participants could remember only half as many commercials as watching programs with neutral content (2002).

Even health programs create fear. Who does not know the hypochondriac fears leafing through a clinical dictionary? Medical knowledge can trigger severe conflicts. If we detect a lymph node swelling we may ranging from the fear of suffering an immunodeficiency or only a trivial infection. Medical practitioners confirm that numerous patients appear in their offices after the presentation of disease symptoms in medical programs. They all believe they are suffering from a disease. They often require the featured new examination methods and therapeutic measures. That leads to a cost explosion in the illness care but bears no means to maintaining health. We better think about how to create beautiful water crystals and better live according to it. Whenever we are frightened and stressed out, the water responds structureless. Above all, it dehydrates the body excessively.

By the power of the mind, we are the
creators of our world; so, we better
participate in a perfect creation!

The cause study of the following water-deficiency diseases shows that we are by no means powerless. Thus, we better trust nature and protect us from the spirit of fear, moral decay, toxic and dead drinking water as well as pesticides, chemical drugs and other evils of our questionable civilization! We must question everything today. Behind every scandal, any prohibition or new disease might be interests opposite of ours. Fearful people are most exploitable. Just think of the purchasing power of shocking headlines!

Repressing and denying our fears makes them become our enemy, and we are their victims. Let's explore them as a product of thought. We've all experienced that fear produces irrational behavior. From the history, we know how dangerous a society consisting of anxious individuals can be. We must not be afraid of dwindling habitat and dwindling resources when we have renewable and free energy and strive for sustainability.

* Anxious and stressed out individuals need more water.

* Anxiety is often sent to us via telepathy. We better send them back immediately!

* We better banish all negative thoughts, for they are of no use to anybody.

* Let us remember what we love and not what we fear!

Suffering is based on lacking pure water

Physicians recognize that delirious patients being taken to the hospital clear up after the administration of water. Overall the body works better if it gets enough H_2O.

The body water in a healthy organism is highly structured. This means that via so-called hydrogen bonds numerous water molecules have combined in complex, highly structured molecular groups. Most civilization diseases and almost all old age ailments have to do with the fact that our body water loses structure and we do not consume enough high-energy water. The body dries out and the sorrow over the nightmares called cancer, Alzheimer's and Parkinson's seeps as leaden slime through the cracks of our daily lives. But we are not so helpless and can counteract emaciation, infirmity, and premature aging with simple means. For, as described in Part II, we can easily convert our ordinary tap water in a high structured, healthy wet with water vitalizing devices.

Prof. Dr. Ana Aslan, the famous scientist, who at the age of 91 years was murdered by the regime under Ceausescu, discovered the anti-aging effects of procaine. She was able to prove that the person dies on the collapse of the cell system's ability to regenerate. The reason for this is that with age the cells no longer properly process the supplied nutrients. Consequently, toxic waste accumulates in the cells. As a result, less energy will be provided.

Our slag heaps are the breeding ground for a disease. If we provide our organism regularly with enough activated water and organic sun-ripened food and exercise on a regular basis, we need not be afraid of horrid vegetating.

With the purifying and invigorating wet and regular exercise, even if we only tense and loosen our muscles with isometric, we counteract depression, infirmity, lethargy and premature aging. Nowadays, people are kept alive artificially if they eat junk food. For, preservatives make not only the food but also their consumer durable. But at what price we live longer? Take a look at a nursing home and judge for yourself whether people actually live there or only slowly and agonizingly die. Due to their large molecules preservatives and other artificial substances are hardly absorbed by the cells, deposited and cause problems, especially pain.

We are heading for an aging society, and one thing is certain: the economy cannot much longer afford the medical fiasco. Thus,

Thus, precautionary measures as described in this book, and a holistically oriented medical education is advisable. That could integrate concepts of homeopathy, ayurveda, and natural hygiene. Already established hydro and color frequency treatments could be enhanced. Also, nutritional and environmental issues could be taken up and extended in the curriculum. In each case, the organism as a whole would be in the foreground.

If we are not satisfied with the health care system, we better get smart ourselves and take responsibility for our health!

Instead of listening to any physicians, we better follow Hippocrates, the forefather of all medical doctors! He said: Let food be thy medicine and medicine be thy food. These are fruits, vegetables, grains, nuts, seeds and wild herbs. Junk food such as pizza, hamburgers, hot dogs, ice cream and chocolate are okay at best in minimal doses.

* The body water in a healthy organism is very highly structured and therefore also requires high-energy H_2O.

* Man dies in the collapse of the regenerative capacity of the cell system, caused by many years of slagging and lack of precipitation.

* Lack of water is the leading cause of digestive/metabolic disorders.

Alzheimer's - water shortage leads to plaque

Typical of the Alzheimer's disease are deposits of proteins (amyloid plaques) between the nerve cells of the brain. Also, the neurotransmitter glutamate is significantly increased. How does the neurotransmitter get into the brain? Can it be that the food industry with aspartame, glutamate & Co. drive us mad? Then we need no longer be afraid of Alzheimer's. We simply have to give up junk food and refine our nutritious dishes with natural spices. It is best to include turmeric or curry. Numerous studies around the world confirm that turmeric (contained in curry) slows down the formation of amyloid plaques and acts cell-protective.

We also can keep the brain healthy by drinking pure water, a glass of red wine and eating cold-water fish such as wild salmon containing omega-3 fatty acid and sardines. The freshwater alga Spirulina also contains these essential fatty acids.

www.newsmaxhealth.com/conditions/topic/Alzheimer'sDementia/188

My body reacts to everything that does not belong to it. Since I do not eat manipulated wheat anymore and leave all flavor enhancers out, I had hardly any ailments. Before I often had various symptoms, such as shortness of breath, blurred vision, heartburn, itching, tingling in the back, stomach cramps, diarrhea, migraine headaches, food cravings, numbness in the neck, heart palpitations, hot flashes and lack of concentration.

Since I have an immediate reaction from glutamate, I became aware of the connection between my frequent diseases and glutamate. Not for nothing is glutamate banned in baby food. What is life-threatening for young children, may be less than optimal for adults.

We are to be stupid. A statistic may demonstrate that: Since more than 15 years, the intelligence quotient (IQ) decreases in industrialized countries. Do democratic states need fools? Are democratic states on the decline? In parallel with the decline in intelligence, hyperactivity, ADHD (attention deficit hyperactivity disorder), aggressive and challenging behavior, and learning disorders in children are increasing. More and more people suffer from depression and brain disorders, such as Alzheimer's, Parkinson's and MS.

Klinghardt and Leong found in the brains of Alzheimer's patients instead of the suspected aluminum increased mercury. Thus, amalgam fillings came under suspicion. Then why do not all persons with amalgam fillings get Alzheimer's? I think the reason is also a lack of water. I asked my friend who nursed her husband, an Alzheimer's sufferer for eight years, about his habits. When it came to drinking, she said: Heinz didn't drink much at all, water never. A physician friend, Sabine Bauer, also assured me that she and her fellow doctors are aware of the link between water scarcity and mentality immobility, especially since they could always make the same observations:

Confused people clear up mentally one hour after the administration of a liter of water!

Most doctors advise their patients to drink more. But first, they lack the time to explain this in more detail, and second, they are consciously or unconsciously in a conflict of interest. If all people knew they could only get and stay healthy with water, wild herbs, Spirulina and a natural diet, then who would come to the doctor's office? Therefore, in conventional medicine is less-taught about disease prevention or detoxification of the body. Thence, the clinical dictionaries are getting more and more extensive. The many new diseases that affect mainly the elderly are caused by different toxins that we accumulate in the body over the years. To get rid of them, the organism needs pure water and green stuff. Such medicine is also appreciated by wild animals if they have poisoned themselves.

For each disease, whether the name Alzheimer's, cataract, Parkinson's, cancer or MS, the correct name would be poisoning of the body.

There are different modes of reaction of the organism to various toxins accumulated in the body. People who drink enough pure water, have a good chance to excrete harmful substances.

As already indicated on page 33, the neurosurgeon Russell Blaylock L. found that aspartame and monosodium glutamate (E621) are responsible for serious chronic neurological disorders and other ailments. E621 is contained in yeast extract, milk protein, granulated broth, maltodextrin, flavors, and seasonings.

Aspartame, also sold as AminoSweet, Nutra-Sweet and Canderel, is especially dangerous in the summer.

If the temperature gets above 30°C, the methanol in aspartame converts to formaldehyde and formic acid or methane. Headache, rapid breathing, weakness, nausea, vomiting, and dizziness are the symptoms. In particular, formic acid leads to a metabolic acidosis within 6 to 30 hours and to nerve damage, especially the optic nerve.

My sister in law formerly worked as a dietician in a hospital. She said that all dishes contain flavor enhancers. Also, we can assume that E621 is used in canteens and many restaurants. In most households, we'd find stock cubes and bags of soups with glutamate. My mother also used E621 but had at age 85 still an excellent short-term memory. She drank a lot of activated tap water and took Spirulina regularly. Many dentists also use the blue-green algae for discharging amalgam. In order to prevent Alzheimer's, it would be best to banish E621 from the kitchen and mercury from industrial processing.

Dr. Dietrich Klinghardt's concept to discharge heavy metals with Chlorella, bear's garlic, and coriander is world-famous. Such people are, strangely enough, seldom invited to shows about Alzheimer's! Apparently, so that the status quo will never have to change. A shockingly high number of former high politicians now act as lobbyists for the pharmaceutical industry.

Dr. Joachim Mutter and his fellow researchers from the Uniklinik Freiburg were able to show in animal experiments that minimal amounts of mercury have already triggered Alzheimer's typical nerve changes. Also, studies of the dental condition of Alzheimer's patients suggest that the mercury causes Alzheimer's. (Mutter et al. 2010). Klinghardt 1996 and Leong et al. Observed in 2001 that mercury is released from amalgam fillings and deposit in the brain.

If we investigate ourselves, we can observe that patients with Alzheimer's or dementia drink hardly pure water.

The sham battles of traditional medicine reminds me of Cervantes' Don Quixote. Do doctors really think they could rid the brain of deposits with a tablet? The only thing that works, is the glass of water with which the tablet is washed down. The intellectual organ shrinks by up to 20% in the course of Alzheimer's disease. The brain cells just need more water, namely clustered water because of its immense absorption power in the cells. It can regenerate the cells, remove toxic deposits and flush these out.

We all know the example of the wrinkled apple: Let's put it into the water for a while, and it is again full and smooth. So it does not require any complicated gray cells arithmetic to figure out that a shrunk cell will be full and supple again by pure drinking water. But as I said, we increase the amount of water better by and by as not absorbed water otherwise might get into the lungs.

All members of Alzheimer's patients try better the administration of pure water and full baths as therapy!

Dr. med. Anthony M. Schmid suggests that extra clean water flushes our brain. Especially since the cells of our intellectual organ contain far more water than the rest of our body cells. With plenty of pure water, our thinking can be crystal clear. The problem is that older people often refuse to drink plenty of water. First, because they do not know how important it is. On the other hand, they do not want to go to the bathroom often at night. However, since the elimination cycle finishes at 12:00 and in the afternoon the body barely cleans, it makes more sense anyhow to drink more water until noon. At this time, the pollutants are best discharged.

If Alzheimer's patients refuse to drink water, a family doctor can show members how to attach infusions so their relatives can use the vital wet during sleep. We better do something so that the following prediction of the Kiel Institut für Gesundheitssytemforschung will not be confirmed:

Compared to an estimated 1.5 million people with dementia in 1997, in 2030, up to 2.5 million are expected.

(DER SPIEGEL 1/2001)

We better help to bring patients and their families to light that we can counteract this prognosis! We better spread the truth about water deficit and insufficient excretion of toxins as the main cause of diseases with the following study:

Canadian researchers found that minute amounts of mercury, far less than released from amalgam fillings, have already nerve-damaging reactions. Minimal traces of mercury are sufficient to cause amyloid plaques, typical for Alzheimer's disease. The formerly suspected aluminum and other metals have not led to this reaction. The scientists could demonstrate seven different pathological protein markers that are responsible for

Alzheimer's and formed in the presence of very small amounts of mercury as a catalyst (Leong et al. 2001). The researchers have their findings recorded on video that we can download from the Internet:

www.mercuryexposure.info

As I said, we can discharge the highly toxic mercury with the microalga Spirulina. That has already been established in 1988, by Japanese scientists under the direction of Yamane. Algae are also known to release other pollutants, even radioactive substances. That is apparently the reason why Japanese people compared to residents of western industrial nations suffer far less of Alzheimer's among other modern epidemics. And this despite the dropped atomic bombs in 1945! You ask why? The Japanese integrate 10-15% algae (Spirulina, Chlorella, Arame, Dulce, Kelp, Nori, Wakame, etc.) in their diet.

Based on Klinghardt's recipe, with this

Pesto for discharging toxins

we can carry out regular cleanings of our organism:

2 - 3 bunch cilantro herb or wild herbs
       wash and liquefy together with
½ cup olive oil, some water and
½ tsp Himalayan crystal salt in a blender.
       Fill in a screw-cap jar, bind with
1 tablespoon Spirulina and
1 tsp brown algae powder (kelp).

* H_2O deficiency causes the Alzheimer's typical shrinkage of the brain.

* Daily 1½-2 liters of pure water (spring water or energized tap water) are best to prevent the deposition of metals in the brain.

* In the morning, the body excretes the most. Therefore, we better drink a lot before noon.

* Mentally confused people quickly clear up after the administration of one liter of H_2O.

* Water brings vital nutrients to the cells and provides for the elimination of harmful substances.

* Minimum amounts of mercury lead to nerve-damaging reactions.

* Algae discharge the liquid metal mercury (amalgam) from the body.

Arthritis – proper purging helps with joint pain

Arthritis is not a disease, but rather a generic term for a combination of symptoms, usually caused by sweet, fat and white paste food and a lack of clean water, raw food, and exercise. Joint pain indicates that the related region of the body lacks water. Pain pills mask the underlying cause and may induce extra damage. Drinking sufficient amounts of water and some crystal salt can help better.

Millions of patients in pain are considered chronically suicidal; hundred of thousands take their life each year because nobody can help them and they are emotionally in a critical state.

With inflammatory pain, we avoid eating animal protein, especially pork, and sausages and drink plenty of pure water. Also, deposits in the joints are based on a dehydrated body condition. By supplying 6 to 8 glasses of water (1 to 2 glasses of tap or still water ½ hour before each meal), arthritis can be cured.

Let's try taking the natural painkiller Spirulina, 3 to 5 tablets with a big glass of water. The blue-green alga alga is a miracle cure for anti-inflammatory pain (Meyer 2002, 2006, 2011, 2014).

* Lack of water leads to deposits and inflammatory pain.

* We better first test whether a glass of water without a tablet relieves the pain.

* Spirulina is a known remedy against pain, based on rheumatoid arthritis.

Asthma/Allergy: too many burdens, too little water

Shortness of breath, persistent cough, skin diseases and other allergic reactions have to do with environmental pollution, congestion, and chronic stress. Because compared to the 50s and 60s, when there was only 1% of asthmatics and allergy sufferers, the spread of asthma and allergy currently gets totally out of control.

Certain substances (allergens) can trigger severe respiratory distress. Airway obstruction causes seizures as a result of spasm, edema or excessive mucus secretion. Dr. Batmanghelidj assumes that asthma is an indication that the body has increased the histamine production, distributed to the nerve endings. This neurotransmitter controls the water metabolism and distribution of water in the body. Is there too little water in the body, more histamine is needed and therefore distributed in order to protect water resources. Since it has been found a higher histamine content in the lung tissue of asthmatic patients, the doctor assumes that they do not drink enough water and concludes that asthma can be treated by drinking water regularly. Asthmatics should ask themselves: Do I drink enough water without gas? According to Batmanghelidj, drinks leading to addiction such as coke, coffee, tea, wine, and beer dry the body even more out.

We better test pure water as a therapeutic!
If we do not do research ourselves,
who else should have an interest in
exploring water as a remedy?

However, the mental aspect of allergic asthma should be considered. Namely is at stake our personal approach, according to which we choose to respond to the continuously flowing environmental stimuli. The more we open up, the greater the flow of information, but also the task to be mastered. If we burden us more than it is good for us, we inflate and at the decisive moment are not in a position in time to blow off steam, so exhale enough. My mother was the prime example of a kept in suspense asthmatic. At age 80, she made the garden and pottery. She painted, knitted, darned and sewed with speedy hand for children, grandchildren, and great-grandchildren. She traveled, lead and attended seminars, honorary offices, choir, gymnastics, dance groups, agenda-21. And she tried never to miss an informative program: a jack of all trades. We also can be out of breath when we are over-whelmed by love or restricted in our freedom. As a teenager, I suffered for several months from shortness of breath, as my friend did not want to let me go. X-ray and other tests gave negative results. Only during my studies I came up with the cause of my problems in adolescence. In addition to people, animals or plants cannot (any longer) fit our concept of consciousness and cause shortness of breath or other allergic reactions such as sneezing, edema, rash or diarrhea. Certain foods can cause an asthma attack, often with increased mucus production. In such a case, I am symptom-free after sucking some Spirulina tablets or drinking a glass of water.

A year ago, I found out that I also suffer from a gluten allergy. Since then, I quit eating wheat and the frequent diarrhea stopped. My body seems to resist anything unnatural. Man has once again called the creation into question, by extremely crossing the wheat, but completely ignored the fact that the change of its biochemical structure could affect the human body. Or was the grain manipulated to shorten our lives because the preservatives in food prolong life de facto? Let us protect ourselves better with pure water and beware of consumption of all foods that are addictive and cause symptoms.

* The lungs of asthmatics have an increased content of histamine, which controls the water metabolism and protect water resources.

* Too much information and too many tasks cause that we are no longer in a position at a crucial moment, to omit.

* Asthmatics need rest, meditation, breathing exercises and plenty of water.

* The increasing occurrence of gluten allergy could be a reaction against engineered crops.

Immunodeficiency - micro-clustered water strengthens the body's defense

Are you daily taking medication or consume chemical and artificial substances in the ready-to-eat meals? If you do not provide for sufficient elimination of these impurities with purified water, you risk suppressing the immune system. Permanent electrical stress, radioactive contamination, as well as physical and mental stress, cause our immune system to impair. The skin, cells, blood, bone marrow, lymphatic and endocrine system, tonsils, appendix, spleen, liver, and nerves no longer function correctly. The immune system gets out of balance since the blood is getting thick and sticky. The water balance regulating neurotransmitter histamine is also involved in the defense system of the body against microorganisms and foreign substances (proteins and chemicals). In a healthy water balance, these functions run unnoticed. But,

if the body dehydrates,

there is an exaggerated water regulating activity of the histamine!

In addition, the immune system stimulates histamine-producing cells to distribute an increased amount of this tissue hormone and neurotransmitter, which is intended for entirely different purposes. Animal studies confirm that the histamine production decreases with a daily increase in water supply. Hence, we better drink enough of the life-sustaining blue gold, the basis of all body fluids.

* Pure water keeps the blood thin.

* The lower the viscosity of the blood, the better the immune cells work.

* If there is sufficient water supply, the body must produce less of the water regulating the histamine.

Cancer - disturbance in the water balance

With this civilization disease, the immune system can be strengthened by drinking plenty of fresh water. Pure water stimulates the immune cells. The activated macrophages (large phagocytes) can thus form the tumor necrosis factor that dissolves selectively tumor cells.

The cancer activity develops at different levels. For example, cancer may arise from any pending issues or loneliness, frustration, fear and lack of love. Also, environmental toxins, too much animal protein, and geopathic zones can cause cancer. Joseph Fraumeni from the National Cancer Institute thinks that 80% of cancers are based on environmental factors such as smoking, poor diet, alcohol, infections and occupational risks.

Here, however, we are talking the considerable carcinogen: lack of living water.

Water controls the cell communication

as well as the metabolic coordination and is,

therefore, for the balance and harmony of the whole system of central importance.

As a result of the increasing contamination of our drinking water with cancer-promoting chemicals, the natural cleaning and regeneration of the body can no longer be achieved. Since tap water is usually energetically dead, the in-house purifying and revival of an essential food is advisable. The purchase of a system for water activation better takes place before the designer couch and a luxury car in order to enjoy the latter goods longer.

In conventional medicine, examining the cell fluid is usually neglected. The Russian biophysicist Karl S. Trincher assumes that not the chemistry of the cell fluid but the network of the water molecules is crucial. Important is not what minerals and other substances a water molecule contains, but how the substances are vibrating together in resonance. Trincher assumes that the destruction of the water structure in the cell leads to the formation of tumors. In the intracellular water, a source of dead cell water comes into being within the living cell water. This foreign body produces a permanent stimulus to the cell to divide. The organized structure of the cell fluid breaks down, the physical structure changes as a whole and degenerated cells begin to proliferate.

A severe water balance and a troubled emotional life are often long lasting precursors of cancer.

In cancer, it is important to supply your body with micro cluster water to relieve the overburdened immune system by the elimination of toxins. We also need to replace the water in the body gradually. End of Nov. 2013, Ouhtit Allal et al. found that Spirulina reduces the new cases of breast tumors from 87% to 13%!

* Living eliminates toxins and regenerates all the cells.

* According to Trincher the collapse of the organized structure of the cell water leads to the formation of tumors.

* Light water and light food such as the blue-green alga Spirulina strengthen the immune system and regenerate the cells.

Parkinson - poisoning of the body

Meanwhile, even the mainstream medicine recognizes that the diet plays a role in Parkinson's and free radicals are associated with the decay process of the brain cells.

A glutamate excess is discussed. In any case, E621 leads to an acidification of the body fluids. Crystallized acids abrade the fine nerve endings, restrict nerve function and interrupt the transmission of impulses from the brain to the muscles. That is due mainly to the fact that we are too far turning away from nature and are too little concerned about purification measures. That also recognizes the Professor of Biochemistry Dr. Günter Gassen of the Technical University of Darmstadt: *Overall, in Parkinson's patients the normal detoxification mechanisms of the body are probably disturbed* (2004).

Those who drink little, cannot detoxify. The correct treatment would be pure water, vitamin-rich green foods and exercise in the fresh air. But the bad sleep, bad mood, the increased fear of their patients suggest doctors as depression and prescribe antidepressants. For the shoulder and back pain, they recommend spinal disk operations and against constipation they prescribe a laxative.

Many respondents with Parkinson's disease have come into contact with pesticides. Dana B. Hancock and her fellow researchers from the Duke University in Durham, the Miami University and the Udall Parkinson's Disease Research Center of Excellence in Lexington interviewed 615 people. 319 were PD patients and 296 healthy volunteers and their families. They were asked about the frequency of their contact with pesticides. The result of the survey was clear: Those who during their life sprayed pesticides to plants or insects of more than 200 days doubled the risk of disease. In particular, it was herbicides and insecticides that increased the likelihood of illness (2008). However, other factors such as smoking or coffee consumption also play a role.

www.biomedcentral.com/1471-2377/8/6

It would be wise to ask Parkinson's patients about their diet, also whether and how much pure water they drink. If we investigate ourselves, we simply get to the cause of diseases. Namely the lack of excretion of toxins due to too little pure water. We better force ourselves to drink more and often use a pesto to wash out poisons (see page 79). We best avoid all beverages and foods with artificial sweeteners.

In Germany alone, agricultural products are fogged annually by about 40,000 tones of pesticides. Therefore, we are all at risk unless we finally go for organic products!

Other risk factors include drugs and mass vaccinations. But there may also be a potential neuroprotective agent for Parkinson's disease. In 2011, Xiang Gao and his team of researchers from Harvard Medical School in Boston published an online study. That suggests that the administration of ibuprofen, two or more times a week, can apparently decrease the inflammation in the brain associated with Parkinson's. In any case helps the water to eliminate the anti-inflammatory drug, too.

* Parkinson's disease is another state of a poisoned system and a lack of excretion of harmful substances.

* Overacidified humors sand down the delicate nerve endings, restrict the nerve function and interrupt the transmission of impulses.

* Parkinson is associated with pesticides, drugs, and mass vaccination.

* The pollutants can be discharged with large amounts of structured water and algae.

* If in your lifetime you spray herbicides or insecticides more than 200 days you double the risk of developing Parkinson's disease.

* Harvard researchers assume, 2 to 3 weekly doses of ibuprofen reduce the brain inflammation associated with Parkinson's disease.

V. FREE ENERGY FOR FREE PEOPLE

None are more hopelessly enslaved than those who falsely believe they are free.

Johann Wolfgang von Goethe

Schauberger's home-energy station

As one of the most famous founders of the free energy, Viktor Schauberger wanted to reveal his fellow humans news on the ancient knowledge of the nature of the water. But the ranger, full of devotion to nature, was fought bitterly throughout his life. He died hurt, lonely and wretched.

If his findings would be generally accepted, we'd have healthy water and could get from water and the air unlimited, clean and almost free energy. We needed to replace only the current death technique of explosion by the biotechnology of implosion to solve the biggest problems facing humanity. And this is also the reason, anything that would make us independent of the energy, is suppressed.

Acting on his maxim *understand and copy nature*, at his creative observing, Schauberger saw the trouts standing or jumping through waterfalls. He noticed something that goes totally against the learned physics. The swirl in the streams seek the path of the least resistance and unleash its forces. With their engines resembling gills, they sucked themselves effortlessly through the water. The entropy has to do with the disorder of a system. Schauberger realized a law of technology of inanimate or by humanly directed nature: things strive to pass in disarray. In contrast, the living nature was able to create order out of itself and to combine energy rather than dissipate. Realizing this, the idea of developing an elementary technique originated.

Schauberger used the ability of water to accelerate in vortex form itself and developed a small power station for home use. He called it suction turbine or spiral because the water is flowing down through ram horn-shaped pipes up to the speed of sound. By the developing thrust, the generator is ultimately driven. It is thereby generating more electricity than necessary to get the water upward again. The trout gills mutated in the so-called Repulsine. This flying disc like the trout sucks itself in the waterfall through the air upwards. The unit applies the air, water, CO_2, some supplements, copper and other catalysts.

The military was interested in Schauberger's inventions. But for the civil sector they were never intended. A home-acting power plant would have meant the independence of the people of oil, gas, and coal. Of course, the ones that earned so well on the minerals, could not allow that. The rights to his inventions ended up with an American concern. Adhesion contracts prohibited him to continue with his research for the rest of his life.

Energy turnaround due to the practical usability of the space or ether energy

What is free energy? The Chinese call it Qi, the Japanese Chi, the Hindus Prana. The ancient Greeks called it the energy of the vacuum, Nikola Tesla scalar waves, Wilhelm Reich Orgone. Others call it tachyon or cosmic energy. Here we call the free energy space or vacuum energy, from the Latin *vacuus* as empty space. But no matter how we want to name it, we better do everything we can so that humanity can finally use the infinite space energy.

The fossil fuels uranium, oil, coal, and gas pollute our environment and are finite. They will be exhausted in a few decades. The German electricity demand was met in 2012 to about 25% by renewable energy. In 2010, in the US renewable energy supplied 8%.

http://en.wikipedia.org/wiki/Energy_in_the_United_States

84

Renewable energy is an expensive affair. Professor Dr. Claus W. Turtur of *Ostfalia Hochschule für Angewandte Wissenschaften* in Wolfenbüttel developed a low-cost alternative. On the internet, we can follow his many brilliant lectures. Turtur has been working for years, in order to make the zero-point energy of electromagnetic waves of the quantum vacuum, just vacuum or space energy, usable. These are electromagnetic waves, such as solar power, only in a lower quantum state. This energy is available forever. In America and Australia, space energy machines work with official test certificates by TÜV Rheinland and other major testing organizations. That means that the use is not a technical problem, but a human or political one. Only if this sole difficulty is overcome, the space energy can gain a foothold. And since it does not pose any health risks, it is environmentally friendly, inexhaustible, widely available and extremely economicals, we should put pressure on our elected representatives.

The zero-point energy goes back to the fathers of quantum theory. What Heisenberg, Bohr, and Schrödinger had proven for individual oscillators, Hendrik Casimir had transferred over in 1948 to electromagnetic waves. For half a century, his vacuum energy was not taken seriously until finally 1997 Steve Lamoreaux of the US elite university Yale could prove the Casimir effect experimentally. Two at a distance of a few nanometers arranged mutually electrically uncharged metal plates by the force of the waves of the vacuum zero point are pushed towards each other. The mechanical power, measured de facto by Lamoreaux is directly the effect of the zero-point-waves. Since 2005, these forces have manufacturing practical relevance in the computer industry. But can we also use them consistently to drive a machine? Definitely!

Another mostly self-taught researcher in gravitation and space energy is my FB friend Anadish Kumar Pal. For the last five years, the outsider to academics has *been actively engaged in trying to break the theoretical riddle of matching quantum mechanics to gravitation* (http://anadish.webs.com). The medical study drop out is only supported by his family in his research and patenting activities. Pal thinks that the current understanding of gravity linked to the Higgs Field is incorrect, as the current particle and cosmic models do not explain how space itself came into being and what exactly is the 'expansion' of space, research let alone the crucial question of baryon asymmetry.

Alternative drive systems

Free energy machines worked already about 100 years ago, partly *en masse* in the Ford T, the first automobile running off the assembly line. The Pierce Arrow of the genius inventor Nikola Tesla and the Ford Magneto are not a legend! Many true stories, however, are out of selfish motives associated with the area of the conspiracy theory. The rewriting of history is also not just an invention of George Orwell. Back to the Magneto:

Why should the first 40,000 of the successful Ford Model T not have free energy generators by Nikola Tesla built in? After all, the following photos testify to it.

Real free energy solutions that could provide each and everyone energy independence, are suppressed. In contrast, symbolic solutions, such as the wind and solar power, are widely supported, because they do not compete with the status quo. Threatening and murdering creative geniuses must stop! The following internet address contains statistics with the number of exploited and liquidated space energy researchers and another list of the one hundred outstanding clean energy technologies:

http://peswiki.com/energy/Directory:Suppression

I chose the experience report of Bill Williams as an example of the threat of brilliant inventors by narrow-minded egoistic criminals. It is published by Sterlin D. Allan *Pure Energy Systems News*. You can read it as a whole on the link above.

Joe Cell Truck Builder Threatened, Destroys Plans

Bill William had successfully built a truck running on the Joe Cell technology. The power was stronger than in an internal combustion engine. In early April 2006, he shared that with his discussion group on the Internet and that he gets the energy from water and Orgone. Wilhelm Reich, who coined this term for the space energy, died in prison. He had opposed the order of the court to destroy his utensils and all his books. Reich became aware of this vital energy in his research with the microscope.

The Joe Cell is said to draw on Orgone energy. The fairly simple device uses electrically charged water as the "gate" or medium through which the aetheric energy is drawn from the surroundings and transferred to the automobile engine. Bill had pictures and short descriptions written and planned to disclose his success in detail. Since he was massively threatened several days later, he reported on 11.4.2006 about the events:

"I was on my way home Thursday last week [April 6, 2006] and was about 3 miles from the ferry project. I stopped to check the post connection point on the Cell. I was standing in front of my truck, and this late model 2005 or 2006 Ford Explorer pulled up and parked diagonally in front of my truck.

The driver got out of the rig and walked around in front of their rig and approached me. At about the same time, the passenger opened his door.

The driver stated that they wanted me to stop working on all forms of alternative energy. He also stated that we know everything about me, my family, and all my projects past and present.

At about that time, the passenger reached and held up a file that was about 2 or so inches thick. He opened it up and showed me telephone transcripts, emails, messages from the groups that I had belonged to.

They knew where my kids worked, the times they are at work; also my wife's working hours, my grandkids' school, etc. They knew everything.

The driver said that if I did not stop working on this (he then opened up the left side of his jacket and showed his weapon that was holstered) that there would be other consequences.

He also stated that he wanted me to post that I was no longer working in this field and to destroy all my work, i. e. Cells, Drawings, Lab Journals, everything!

At that point, he walked around and got into the rig. I shut the hood and got the hell out of there. They followed me for about 2 miles and then must have turned off somewhere."

After a few days of reflection, Bill decided to comply with the requirements of those who had threatened him. He destroyed the cells, all data, and documents and made his website on which he had posted his plans unusable. Four days after this event, Bill wrote the following message to the group:

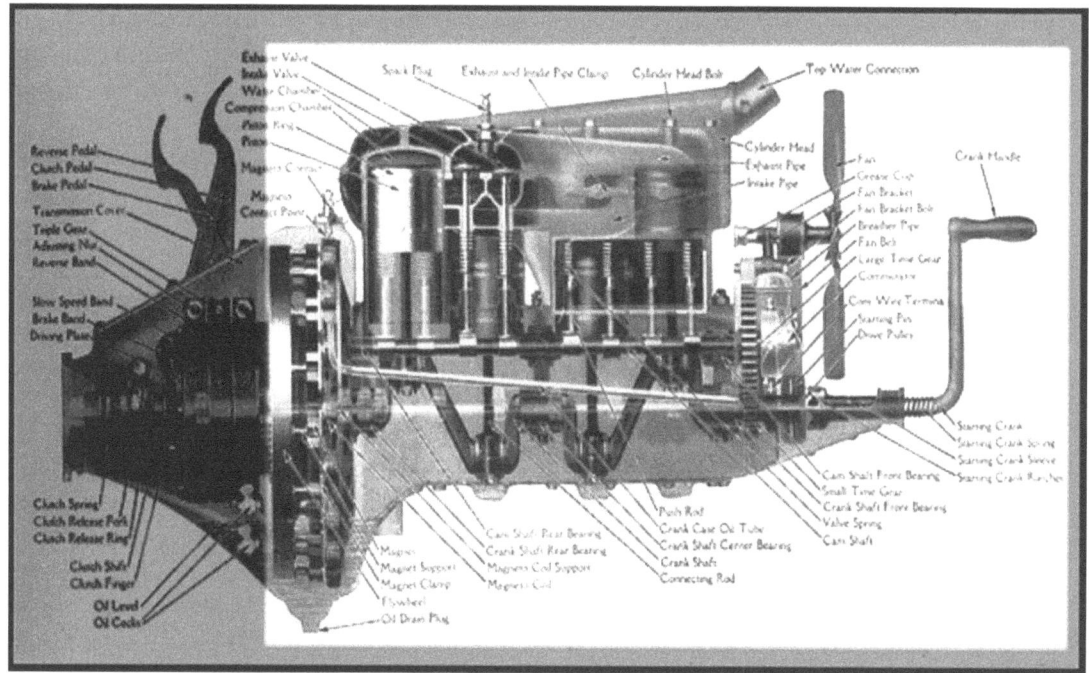

"I thought I was strong but when illness to the family comes into play, I have failed. I am truly sorry. I will not be working in any form of alternative energy field anymore. [...] I destroyed my device tonight along with my written data and lab notes as per specked out."

www.youtube.com/watch?v=DexBoYfDoNw

It makes me sad when the life's work of creative people is destroyed by ignorant contemporaries who are too stupid to recognize the universal contexts.

Tesla's space-energy converter car

The most brilliant inventor of the last century has also been given a raw deal.

Though most references do not credit Tesla with the invention of the radio, he invented it years previous to Marconi. Nobody will deny Nikola Tesla the invention of radar and fluorescent lamps. However, his inventions were often claimed by patents of other inventors. Even if this is not taught in schools because we are deliberately kept stupid, there is still excellent literature about it. So, why should the Tesla car not have existed? Today some tinkerer also know how to use the cosmic energy. And:

If we do not want to dance around the golden calf rushing into disaster, a change in attitude and recognition of the immaterial power and the metaphysics in its whole is inevitable.

Already more than 100 years ago, the inventor of the alternating current managed to draw off free energy from the Universe in abundance. The native Croatian from Serbian-born parents could render from the cosmic rays which surround the earth electrical usable energy through a multi-tube device. This energy he used in his Pierce Arrow that he had converted to an electric vehicle. This luxury car like a Rolls-Royce today, he drove from New York to the Niagara Falls. There he

87

used the power of the falling water for the first AC power plant in the world.

Tesla also crossed America along with a journalist from the Washington Post. This documented journey was undertaken without refueling. Heinrich Jebens, the head and founder of the new German Erfinderhaus (inventor house) in Hamburg is another witness. His son Klaus Jebens describes in his book *Die Urkraft aus dem Universum* the specifics of his father's ride in the fall of 1930 with the Tesla car, including technical details. He also describes similar developments from three other inventors in detail.

However, Tesla's free energy generators should have been installed much earlier in mass production cars. Hard to believe?

The Ford Magneto free-energy motor

The photos of the magneto and the Ford magneto-Line station suggest that the legend is true. The original manual with a section on the magneto is increasing the evidence. The numerous Ford T Magneto building instructions and photos that I got from the Google Boys indicate that we could have used environmental safe power more than hundred years ago! 1908, the first handmade Ford Model T was finished. The *Tin Lizzy*, the first car produced on an assembly line, contained a suitable autonomous operation flywheel magneto. Looking at the photos, who would deny that in the first 40,000 cars Tesla's free energy generators were installed?

At the beginning of the 20th century, the auto industry was in transition. Since Tesla developed a free energy electric car and successfully presented it, nothing would have spoken against to build in his space-energy converters. Henry Ford had been negotiating with the oil industry, but also flirted with alcohol or hemp oil as fuel; also with the free-energy motor of Tesla.

Mineral oil was the most lucrative. Sup-

plies once seemed unlimited. However, Ford wanted to avoid cartel or monopolistic situations and hedge against price gouging by oil companies. That's why his workers were still building in the first 40,000 Ford T models a part of the Tesla drive.

"The Magneto, who supplied the engine with ignition voltage, should after assembly of horseshoe-shaped cobalt-Samarito magnets be able to deliver 30 hp free energy. There was a hostile takeover attempt of the competition. Ford was said to have averted it by threatening to send the information necessary for completion of the Tesla drive and the available components (more magnets) to the owner of the 40,000 cars."

http://julius-hensel.com/2010/10/freie-energiehenry-ford-blockte-teslas-magneto

This deliverance is not regarded as secure, but with a little luck, we can bid on an intact Magneto on Ebay. On the net, there is also a repair help for the magneto at:

  Ford T Center: Magneto-original photos;
  ibid., interactive graphics

The magazine cover on page 90 shows another generator, driven only by a magnetic motor. There are a lot of free energy machines. The names of potential inventors flood the book market and the internet that it is easy to lose track. Many turn out to be charlatans. That impedes the entire sector of space energy research. Proponents of space power are just as loud as the doubters. I think that many frauds are actually on duty to stop the great revolution of energy supply. Therefore, I will focus on some existing, functioning vacuum energy converters that have been officially verified.

The in a barn discovered first Porsche P1 Year 1898 was an electric car that managed with one battery charge a range of 80 km and 35 km/h! It makes you think that this is already 117 years ago!

such as water, solvents, battery acid, coke and others. Pantone was also severely threatened within 24 hours after the broadcast by political and economic circles. He had feared for his life and, therefore, kept a low profile, focusing on pure research in the following years to refine and miniaturize the device. Today Pantone has several marketable plasma generators in the program. These convert the fuels specifically and optimize the combustion process in engines considerably. Pantone collaborates with various other inventors and has approximately 50 distributors.

http://pesn.com/2010/07/29/9501680_GEET_pl asma_fuel_processor_kit_now_in_production/

The GEET Plasma Reactor by Paul Pantone

The US company GEET (Global Environmental Energy Technology) develops and trades environmentally friendly engines. As early as 1985, Paul Pantone, a brilliant inventor, introduced the first prototype of a GEET device on the TV news. Energy efficient it ran on waste oil and various additives

The Keppe motor for small purses

The Brazilian philosopher Dr. Norberto Keppe claims to have developed the most efficient and least expensive electric motor in the world. On this motor, applies the principle of electromagnetic resonance to optimize. Its development is based on the hypothesis formulated in his book *The New Physics Derived from a Disinverted Metaphysics*. The main hypothesis states, that energy does not come from matter as the physics, are teaching, but all matter is composed of a primary energy, the essential or scalar energy. That exists in inexhaustible quantities throughout the universe. The Keppe Motor has a US patent protection as a registered trademark. It uses five times less energy than a conventional electric motor. We can reproduce it:

www.keppemotor.com/ge/index.php

The Terawatt overunity magnetic motor

The California-based company *Terawatt Research* developed a technology to produce power for the production of electricity based on interactive magnetic oscillation (IMO). Terawatt demonstrated IMO and produced workable designs of an apparatus which will generate energy. They state they are "harnessing the energy of intermolecular fluctuations." (www.terawatt.com)

The efficiency of this overunity magnetic motor is verified by TÜV Rheinland of North America and Underwriters Laboratories Inc. At least three times more energy is produced from the system than what is required to drive the system.

Professor Turturs space-energy converter

The physicist and basic researcher Professor Claus W. Turtur wanted to investigate and measure that thing with the free energy himself in the laboratory. He devised a private experiment. He conducted the study at the Otto-von-Guericke University in Magdeburg as a guest scientist. After developing a sound theoretical basis, he built an assembly according to Fig. 1.

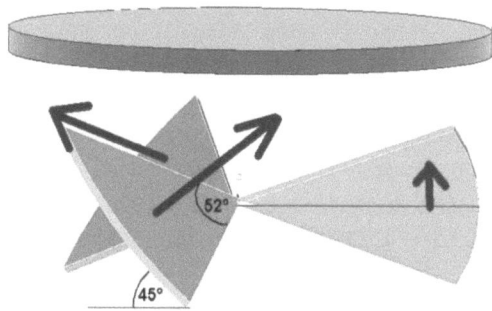

Fig.1:
Electrostatic rotor to convert vacuum energy

The metal disc in the upper part of the image is named field source since it is electrostatically charged. Ergo it generates an electrostatic field. Just as a plastic comb, electrostatically charged by rubbing, attracts scraps of paper, the field source attracts the rotor blades. In this case, the attractive forces pointing in the directions of the arrows. By locating the rotor accordingly, we can prevent that it is flying up to the field source. Rather leads the recti-

linear part of the attraction force to rotating the rotor. And, since the charge cannot drain off the field source, the rotation continues endlessly without a current flow. Thus, the rotor emits mechanical power without consuming electric power. That this is, in fact, the case, Prof. Tutur could prove in cooperation with the University of Magdeburg in the relevant literature published. Here we find an open-source Summary of scientific publications:

http://www.ostfalia.de/cms/de/pws/turtur/FundE/English/

With this change of vacuum energy into rotational mechanical energy, its practical use is first detected at the university level. But it only amounts to a scientific basis experiment. The power is converted in an electrostatic rotor diameter of 64 mm just 150 NW at a voltage of 30,000 V. Since we currently need a power of approximately 1,500 EJ per year, the energy of the people requires completely different systems. Not even the electrostatic principle can be maintained due to a low energy density since the electrostatic field has an insufficient energy density.

The energy content of the magnetic field is substantially higher than that of the electrostatic. Therefore, a vacuum-energy converter with magnetic principle is more sensible.

Prof. Turtur developed a basic calculation method for magnetic vacuum-energy converters of all kinds. Thus, he enabled the construction of such vacuum energy systems. The concept is based on a dynamic extension of the finite element method and hence is called DFEM method. Based on this, Turtur constructed for the purpose of verification of the method in the theory a vacuum energy converter and simulated its operation on the computer. Thereby rotates a permanent magnet in a coil (Fig. 2). This induces a voltage in the coil, which in turn allows an LC

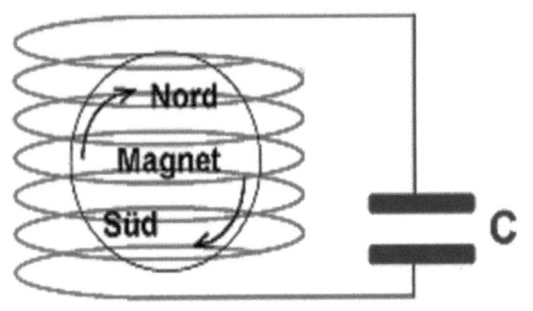

Fig.2: Schematic structure of the electric double mechanical resonant converter

resonant-circuit in oscillation. The field energy of the resonant circuit acts via the Lorentz force back to the magnet. With an appropriate setting of the system, we can convert vacuum energy into kinetic energy of the magnetic rotation and electric energy of the resonant circuit. This allows us to take out of the system mechanical as well as electrical energy. Size and power of the engine are scalable. So we could, f. i., reach dimensions and performance of a commercially available drill. However, it does not require a power supply cable.

In this case, we need to harmonize an electrical and a mechanical resonance. Therefore, the converter is named electromechanical double-resonant converter (EMDR). A collection of scientific publications, also based on this system of inhomogeneous differential equations with variable coefficients, we find here:

http://www.ostfalia.de/export/sites/default/de/pws/turtur/images/1_Series-english-5Articles.pdf

Prof. Turtur would like to implement the developed theory construction for the use of vacuum energy into practice. So far, he is lacking the means. But I'm afraid that as long as the soil can still be looted, the interest in free energy will be limited. The policy has so far complied with the status quo oriented needs of the energy industry. The energy problem cannot be solved by the tentative turn to the wind power and solar cells. All types of energy except the space energy are associated with environmental problems. Therefore, it is our urgent task to ensure that the revolution towards the vacuum energy generators available around the clock finally takes place. They eliminate the need for energy storage and are extremely cost effective. After all, we only need to buy the engine, but no substance as an energy source.

The Dingel water powered car

Earlier than 16 years ago, Daniel Dingel, the Philippine Gyro Gearloose, introduced his converted Toyota Corolla 1.6i that ran 500 km with 5 liters of water. The journalists of the tabloid *Bild* and many others were able to see in the following years that with a speed of up to 200 km/h and 500 rotations per minute idle speed the exhaust consisted only of a few drops of water. How does it work? Not conventionally by explosion of the detonating gas, but by compressed implosive energy space. The engine is cold and running with an enormous amount of pre-ignition. That proves that it could never run with the small amount of oxyhydrogen (detonating gas). The reactor of Dingels water car is a Faraday cage. In it, a normal electrolysis at 12 volts and 5 amps is executed. The electrolysis unit is surrounded by a self-oscillating coil with a few turns. This resonates with the space energy that is reflected back into the interior through the stainless steel container. Consequently, it supplies increased energy to the electrolysis. The engine sucks in the energized and with exhaust air mixed oxyhydrogen. After two-thirds of the compression process, the concentrated ether charge is ignited, and condensed in the form of an implosion.

www.DanielDingel.com

On 06-18-2008, *FAZ* Multimedia put a video on the Dingel car into the net. On 06-23-2008, *N24* reported on the invention of a new drive for cars traveling without additional energy supply with only one liter water about 80 km for circa one hour. It does not matter if we fill up with seawater, mineral water or tea. On 03-16-1999, Dingels car was shown on German television in *N3*. The video you can see on this website:

www.rolf-keppler.de/wasserauto.htm

Here we find the following two and more photos of Daniel Dingel's Toyota Corolla 1.6 i, taken by Wolfgang Czapp.

Rolf Keppler, the descendant of the famous astronomer and astrologer, one of the founders of modern science, talks about his acquaintances Czapp, who lived in the Philippines in 1999/2000. In Manila, he met Daniel Dingel at the Industrial Technology Development Institute in January 2000. Ernesto Luis S., PhD from the Philippine Science and Technology Ministry in Manila organized the meeting with the inventor, who then arrived with his water car.

Also, the BILD reporter Jörg Wigand was on several trips with the water car. Neither in the Metro Manila nor on overland trips on the highway, he did notice any burning smell.

On 10-20-2000, he describes in the *Auto Bild* a mysterious self-made mini reactor in the motor compartment in size of a car battery. The Bild-Team was accompanied by two men, who are familiar with unusual phenomena. Günther E. Brand sponsors inventors. The financial intermediary and risk manager had taken his technical adviser, automotive engineer Dieter Klauke along. They found no evidence of conventional fuels such as gasoline, diesel or gas. Apart from the engine compartment they found in Dingel's car a normal four-stroke four-cylinder. No hidden fuel cell and no apparent signs of burning fossil fuels on board. Had Dingel discovered a phenomenon of the paranormal? There seems to be something very simple, but beyond the reach of normal scientific experience. A new Einstein in the night sky?

Several groups of investors were after shorter test drives with Dingel so convinced of his invention, that they offered him contracts worth millions. His partner Vargas had already signed one of these preliminary contracts, but Dingel did not give his signature. Why? Had he also feared for his family? Why did Dingel, who died in October 2010, refuse any serious tests or the process of patenting? The only several hours test of the engine took place in a BMW branch in Manila. All the local engineers were convinced of the invention. So why did Dingel hesitate with the development? He said: *Because my invention is so simple that anyone would laugh when I publish it. It is based only on common sense, not on an innovative engineering knowledge. How can one take out a patent on such a thing?*

But didn't Dingel, who wanted to be a priest, aim to help humanity? I could imagine that he also knew the universal law of cause and effect. It is that of the seven universal laws which Jesus delivered to the people in

such a manner:

Give, and it will be given to you.

I once experienced this law concretely, when I gave a speech about Spirulina for some 80 country seniors in the Odenwald. When the leader Johann Heim wanted to pay me, I told him to consider the amount as a donation. A little later I was invited to a four-day trip to Berlin, which was circa three times the value.

Was Daniel Dingel fobbed off? Likely with the same reasoning as Viktor Schauberger, who wanted to patent the process of spooling in water vortex, with which he discovered the implosion principle. It was suppressed with the argument that it was not an invention but a law of nature.

How does the Dingel car work? H_2O is decomposed into hydrogen and oxygen with a voltage. Disconnection by 5-10 amperes of current from the normal 12-volt car battery. This hydrogen-oxygen mixture is supplied to the engine. Daniel Dingel said that the system receives 3 amps at 12 volts from the car battery and the alternator. This corresponded to 36 watts. So the car can reach speeds up to 200 km/h. The idle speed amounts to 500 rpm.

The Philippine television had shown the Dingel car several times. One TV reporter drew attention to the series production in the Philippines, starting in early 2001. Large companies, such as VW and TÜV should have called on Dingel. Journalists of the magazine *Auto Bild* repeatedly visited the car of the inspired inventor and took samples from the car exhaust. They could not detect any hydrocarbons in the exhaust gas. Why nothing came of it?

Comment by Rolf Keppler: *Wolfgang Czapp who has seen and filmed the car himself I know personally and he is credible to me. (Stanley Meyer, who is no longer alive, also had a patent on a water car). The energy for the excess energy is of course neither the water nor from the car battery. The decomposition of water by direct current produced no over unity effect (= energy surplus) and will only have an efficiency of 60 to 80%. The excess energy in the Dingel car is probably generated by the fact that the water splits by a high voltage of unknown frequency. The water serves only as a trans-former which transforms the free energy from the high-voltage field in the decomposition of water into hydrogen and oxygen. This principle, which drives the water car by Daniel Dingel is not yet patented worldwide. (In America Dingel has a patent; but such US patents are in dispute useless.)*

Stanley Meyer's water-buggy

A quarter of a century before Daniel Dingel, the American Stanley Meyer discovered the high voltage electrolysis. When in 1973, the oil crisis substantially increased fuel prices, he searched for a way to free his country from the dependence on OPEC. Meyer invented an electrolysis cell with which he split water, using low power, for detonating gas. Stanley Meyer fueled with it a VW engine in a beach buggy. On the following link, we can look at a video in English, in which he introduces his car in detail:

www.youtube.com/watch?v=i1r08iWGqCI

On 06-26-1990, Stan Meyer had his invention patented (4,936,961). The following website

94

shows a 5-page specification. You would think the industry would be keen to take up the prototype in order to develop it into a productive-ready model. This was not the case. Allegedly, the oil industry had offered him $1 billion for all rights. Meyer refused

and after 20 years of development died on March 21, 1998 suddenly in a restaurant. Many assume he was poisoned.

www.wasserauto.de/html/stanley_meyer.html

The following video shows Stan Meyer's buggy driving. Per 100 km, it shall consume 2½ liters of water. Stan has achieved what physicists considered as impossible: water turning into a hydrogen fuel which is enough to drive his buggy with 80 liters of water across the United States. Stan's twin brother Steven accused the same sharks that had poisoned Stan in the restaurant in Grove City, Ohio, have stolen the buggy and the entire experimental equipment a week later. Steven said that his brother was often threatened. He did not want to sell his invention to the Arab Oil Corp.

www.youtube.com/watch?v=a74uarqap2E

How many geniuses have yet to be threatened, tricked or murdered, as Stanley Meyer, Bill Williams, Yull Brown, Andrija, Carl Cella and many others? See also:

http://waterpoweredcar.com/inventors.html

U.S. Patent   Jun. 26, 1990   Sheet 1 of 3   4,936,961

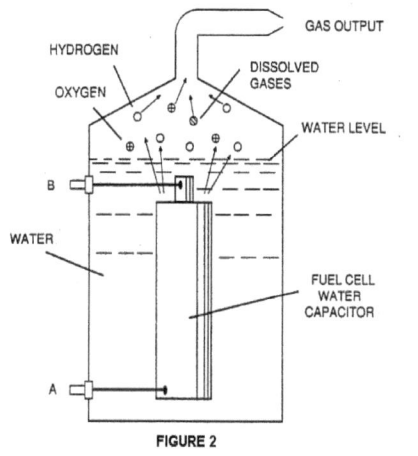

FIGURE 2

U.S. Patent   Jun. 26, 1990   Sheet 2 of 3   4,936,961

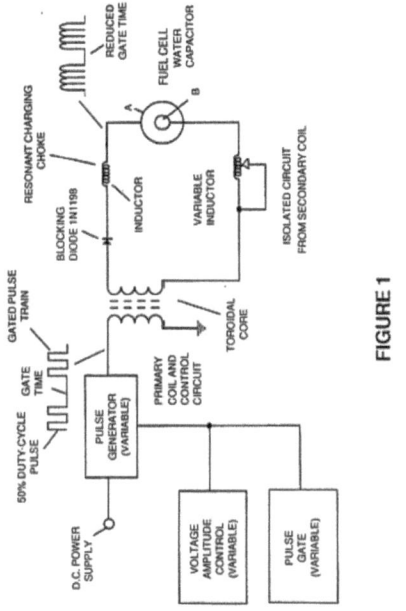

U.S. Patent   Jun. 26, 1990   Sheet 3 of 3   4,936,961

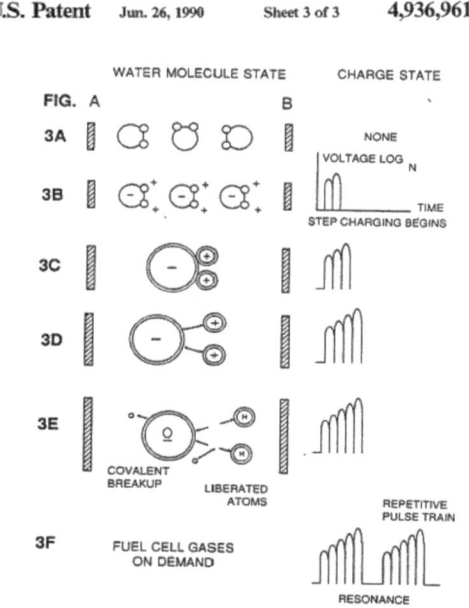

Genepax & Ricketts: More water cars

A prototype of a car that is fueled only with water, also presented the company Genepax on 06-13-2008 on the following video.

www.youtube.com/watch?
v=Jivb7lupDNU#t=40

The Japanese company succeeded in building a fuel cell that works only with water and the air. They call the technology that can split more hydrogen and oxygen than any other membrane electrode assembly or MEA. It works without any other energy or fuel supply. By the company's own account, the car can run 80 km/h with one liter of water.

For how long will we allow the inventions for the benefit of mankind and our planet to be suppressed? For how long will we wait for the mass production of the air- and water-powered cars? There have been prototype cars since the 1920s! When will the MDI air car, presented in 2008/2009 by the Indian car company Tata finally go into production? It is supposed to go into production in 2015 in Sardinia. I'm curious.

http://www.autoevolution.com/news/compresse
d-air-powered-tata-nano-to-get-200-km-125-
miles-range-53879.html

http://users.telenet.be/sarahgrimonprez/didier/ai
rcars/html/actueelENG.html

The electric car company Tesla in California is an acceptable beginning. But who can afford these cars? It's about time that a small inexpensive 5-door car follows.

On 03-12-2012, the Daily News Journal reported on a spectacular ride. Professor Cliff Ricketts from the Middle Tennessee State University (MTSU) had built three hydrogen-powered Toyotas and drove his 8-man escort team 4155 km across the country. The hydrogen is extracted only from filtered tap water via photovoltaic solar panels and electrolysis. The hydrogen gas is then compressed into a circa 2,000-liter tank and extends for considerable 650 km. A 600-tank city car could go 200 km.

www.youtube.com/watch?v=_1Bv99YOGlY

The links to videos about building instructions, specified in various internet articles, no longer exist. Does anybody wonder?

Is the earth energy generator Nilson Barbosa and Cleriston Leal real?

On 12-19-2013, I received an email from Rolf Keppler. A member of his free-energy group had called and told him that he had flown to Brazil due to a Brazilian website. The inspection appointment had been agreed from Germany. In Brazil, he had nobody found as agreed. The phone did not work anymore. Subsequently, the website had been deleted. This aroused my instinct for research. I found out that the two inventors from Imperatriz - MA, Brazil, who had developed their equipment to the production stage and presented at a recent trade show, had been arrested. They were released on bail. Are energy groups and state coffers once again afraid for their financial gain?

The self-propulsion system for power generation of the two inventors shall produce more energy than has to be applied to the initial operation. To start the Gerador Captor Eletrons de Terra (generator for catching earth electrons), we need an initial force of 2% by the local power grid of the amount of energy generated thereafter. In the meantime, the researchers offer their equipment for sale. A relatively small unit shall supply a detached house with free energy. The smallest prototype measures 20x30 x15cm. Its weight is 1.5 kg. It should be able to generate 12.1 kWs with a cargo of 6,000 watts and need just 21 watts input. On 07-07-2013, the device was registered for international patent approval. It shall produce free energy, generated from an initial input of 440 watts approximately 40 kWs at 220 volts, meet the needs of a one family home and costs around € 4,000.

According to Barbosa and Leal, it is an electromagnetic device that brings energy particles in motion, so as to provide immediate-power by electromagnetism.

Here is a video about the invention: www.youtube.com/watch?v=SvcrqODpDY4

The website of the inventors is Portuguese:

http://energiauniversal.eco.br

http://www.ufo-disclosure.net/blog/free-energy-devices-for-march-2014

Under www.overunity.de *Free electricity from the earth*, I found a more detailed explanation of the member 'hartiberlin'. He stated that the device works as a Kapanadze circuit, and positive high-voltage pulses draw negative free electrons from the earth. The earth is indeed through the molten iron in the core, an extremely strong conductor. Lassyles, also a member of overunity.de has apparently invented a free energy device. He sees a parallel to his subject ERU (Elemental Resonance Unit) and assumes that it is a matter of two opposing high-velocity fields, one of which is directed towards the earth, and acts absorptive.

www.overunity.de/1528/eru-elementar-resonanz-unit

I could go on and on with the free energy describing new inventions. Fortunately, not all inventors can be killed. Thus, I'm optimistic that we can be self-sufficient from the energy-sharks soon. At the place of residence of the Brazilians, the devices should have been already sold, apparently the reason for their detention. Or could they be arrested because the equipment sold does not work? Either way, the thrill remains. It is certain that working free energy systems exist. Also, the above video should demonstrate the operability of the earth energy generator. Patents are pending in 198 countries. Shouldn't that indicate that it works?

Strong Skondin magnetic motor scooter

The efficiency of the above-described devices can be questioned. The same applies to Muammer Yildiz's Magnetic Motor and others. But in Russia, we can admire a true ultra-efficient electronic magnetic motor on a bicycle, tricycle, and wheelchair. It can even tow a car as we can see in the video of a Dutch television!

http://sunny-farm-news.blogspot.pt/2010/09/der-magnet-motor.html

We also find the detailed European patent application. If this page should be removed, following the video uploaded on 25.4.2009 by Peter Cernjavski:

www.youtube.com/watch?v=L1rilJFviVM

If the current slump in the oil prices is initiated by the Saudis and USA to taking out Russia, a mass production of magnetic motor vehicles may be a proper answer.

Leslie Szabó's 300 MW power plant

Prof. Leslie Szabó advertises a 300 MW power plant on his company website. It allegedly heats 280 homes. Inge and Adolf Schneider heading the Swiss Jupiter-Verlag recently told me that it's still a vision of the future: *The magnetic motor, Prof. Szabó presented in the laboratory, has an efficiency of 130%. That is for scientific judgment alone an impossibility, but can still be measured. Mathematical calculations for the scale-up on such motors, by independent professors, show that completely autonomously running 300-MW power plants are possible.*

The Jupiter-Verlag (www.jupiter-verlag.ch) regularly informs about working magnetic motors on their website www.borderlands.de and in the *NET-Journal, the only German-language magazine about free energy technologies.*

Worldwide invent clever tinkerers drive types, which allow free mobility and energy supply without polluting the environment. But the practical use is controversial. Are narrow-minded egoists of the energy and money monopoly blocking this environmentally friendly free energy? Or are we kept dumb because we are not yet mature enough for the knowledge of the spiritual forces of the free energy? But if the world should recover, it will be necessary to free us from the hassle of oppression. Realizing that we are enslaved, makes us not automatically free. But we can defend ourselves and conquer our freedom piece by piece. We are the people! If we realize this, we recognize our duty as citizens to take action against injustice and environmental degradation.

Concluding remarks

Would it not it be wonderful if we could all progress rapidly on the path of knowledge? This would be possible if more and more scientists at the research got rid of the blinkers and explored the world without prejudice like kids. Children are our true philosophers and researchers on which we better orient ourselves. They always want to see behind the apparent world.

Would scientists unreservedly and consequently use all the instruments available to them, we could leave the destructive way on which we approach the abyss. This would require that the upper castes would allow a consciousness that makes it possible to recognize spiritual energy as what it really is. If we consider certain phenomena as instructional media, we need no longer fear them as a threat.

The energy revolution has to start soon anyway. The dwindling resources make it imperative that we deal with the cosmic laws. Because these are capable of solving the energy problems of mankind and prevent future conflict potentials. But as long as there are still bombs exploding in cars or the inventors end up in prisons or mental hospitals or accept large sums of money to make their inventions disappear, we will have to be the ones to approach the inventors. We can make them produce short runs and distribute them everywhere. We also can sign existing Zero-point-power online petitions or start new ones. If we desire cars running on compressed air, water or solar and exert pressure, we can gradually cause change

with our buying power. Maybe the creative people will find out that the millions, they expect to earn can flow slowly but surely when they start small and place their models in different places. Ground Gross has done just that. His award winning water activator is already being sold in many countries. That reminds me of my colleague James Redfield. In 1993, he published his novel *The Celestine Prophecy*. The first 10,000 copies he sold out of the trunk of his car. In 2005, the Time Warner publishing had already sold 20 million books! If we're afraid of being attacked, manipulated or even killed, we can manufacture our inventions quietly at home and sell to the distributors, as Peter and Isabel Gross do, with their Aqua Lyros system for water activation.

Fear is also the reason why I freed Prof. Turtur from his promise to write the foreword. He indicated that he had received threats. His wife is always panicky if he is late and expects the worst.

On 09-11-2013, I lit a white candle for my friend Marita Rohde. I researched the internet for everything I could find about the murder of 3,000 people. I read about 200 US architects who doubt the presented version of the collapse of the WTC towers. In the German economy news, I read that the majority of Americans believe in a controlled demolition. But what cheered me to write a blog article, was the report of a politician. In the early 80s, he served under Helmut Schmidt and belonged to the Bundestag for 25 years. According to the conceptual model of the former Federal Minister for Research and Technology Andreas von Bülow, the Bush administration or standing behind it powerful circles have had more than 3,000 people killed. Why? To have persuasive arguments for the great-power ambitions serving military operations such as in Iraq and Afghanistan. This thesis based Bülow, among others, on the following alleged fact: Four weeks after 9-11, former NATO commander Wesley Clark stopped by his old comrades from the general staff. Excited, they had told of their mission to bring about a change of governments in Iran, Iraq, Libya, Algeria, and a number of other states within five years. All revolutions, also the Arab Spring, were initiated from the outside.

Mrs. Turtur read my online report based on these accounts. She then worried about her husband even more because of the planned preface. I deleted the report three days after the 12th anniversary of 9-11. Instead of a professor's preface, now my readers can learn something about the disturbing everyday life of an inventor, highly unpleasant for energy monopolists. It must be hard to live like that. Therefore, I appeal to your fairness and generosity and ask you to sign the petition:

http://akademieintegra.wordpress.com/2013/04/2 9/petitionsaufruf-raumenergie-claus-turtur/

Hence, we can achieve that Prof. Turtur will be eligible for funding. His free energy system, which he already installed with his family's own funds over the bath tub could be accessible for us in a larger format. I would be glad if space energy could come in all households as already Tesla had planned 100 years ago. Why did he not achieve it? It is always the same. The ominous money business continually hinders prosperity for all.

End of Dec 2014, Prof Turtur asked me if Doris Day had not enough connections to get research projects to work. I answered that she is so involved in her animal foundation DDAF and at age 90 she might not have the drive for something else. But since I'm going to send her my new book *Migrant Birds on Wheels*, I promised to suggest it in my letter to Doris. Claus Turtur wrote back: *The animals are also better off if people stop to destroying the earth with the energy policies.* I secured to send Doris the entire conversation. The Prof urged again: *If we do not stop destroying the earth, then soon a lot of people and very many animals will die. We call it a population cut.* With the space energy, I would like to avoid exactly this population cut. I promised the Prof to send Doris the entire conversation. And of course, as soon as this book is published, Doris gets a copy. So she can read that again, too.

It is time to wake ourselves up with a jolt! Please, don't just put down the book and think: Well, it'll be all right! We better take care that Tesla, Reich, Schauberger, Meyer, Williams and all the others who have been treated badly or were murdered get their due recognition. Let's not allow the genius to be furthermore trampled and the people stultified? Please, address your elected representatives that brilliant minds don't have to resign, as once Victor Schauberger when he wrote his famous farewell letter. It was the last before his death:

> *I'm going back to my forest, in order to die there in peace. The whole of science and all its appendages are just a bunch of thieves who hang like puppets on strings and have to dance to any tune that their well hidden slave masters consider necessary.*

We may add the main body of politicians. When will people who strive for short-term gains realize that in the end they have to live with the damage they cause? When will they realize that reincarnation and karma are no esoteric blah blah, but the universal law of cause and effect. The Apostle Paul expresses it like this: What man sows, he will reap. Today we would say: The karma strikes back. Under this law, there is neither guilt nor the common blame-the-other game, nor coincidence or luck. There are only cause and effect which can be many centuries and incarnations apart. Luck, bad luck, and chance are only symbols of the unrecognized law.

I wish you that you can now acquire all the luck in the world through your brilliant creative power.

Acknowledgments

It takes a community to educate authors. It takes a publisher to publish writings. Exemplary houses offer authors the economic conditions to continue writing. I thank *Books on Demand* in Norderstedt for the generous conditions and the excellent handling.

Heartfelt thanks to my community, friends and family. Many of my circle of life are already on the other side and help me in different ways. Thank you!

I am especially grateful to Dr. agr. Renate Kaiser-Alexnat for her contribution *Woad water wonder*. I also thank Inge and Adolf Schneider for a correction in the free energy part and Prof. Dr. Claus W. Turtur for generously providing his work. Isabel Gross, Rolf Keppler, Thomas Mattmann and Wolfgang Czapp I thank for materials and suggestions.

Last but not least, I'd like to express my special thanks to Ernst F. Braun for his creative work and the permission to publish his wonderful water crystal photos. I also thank for the following friendly *Water Being 2014*. I interpret it as a symbol of fertility and resurrection and would like to give courage to all my readers. The seeds are coming up.

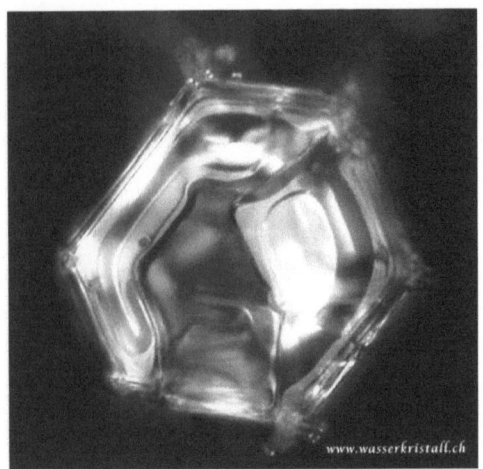

www.wasserkristall.ch

References

Blaylock, Russell L.: Health and Nutrition Secrets: That Can Save Your Life: Harness Your Body's Natural Healing Powers, Albuquerque, USA 2006

Burggrabe, Hilmar, Strauß, Markus: Trinkwasser und Säure-Basen-Balance, Weil der Stadt 2009

Buschmann Bj, Bonacci, AM: Violence and sex impair memory for television ads, J. Appl. Psych, 2002 Jun; 87(3):557-64

Capelli, B. Cysewski, G.: The World's Best Kept Health Secret: Natural Astaxanthin, 3rd Ed. 2013

Chiu, HF et al. Effect modification by drinking water hardness of the association between nitrate levels and gastric cancer. J Toxicol Environ Health A 2012;75(12):684-93

Coats, Callum: Naturenergien verstehen und nutzen. Viktor Schaubergers geniale Entdeckungen, Omega-Verlag Düsseldorf 1999

Emoto, Masaru: Die Botschaft des Wassers. Burgrain 2010.

Edde, Gérard: Das Heilbuch der fünf Elemente. St. Goar 1992, S. 11f.

Eshak, E. S. *et al*: Soft drink intake in relation to incident ischemic heart disease, stroke, and stroke subtypes in Japanese men and women: the Japan Public Health Centre-based study cohort I.October 17, 2012

Feijó Fde M, Ballard, C.R. *et al.*: Saccharin and aspartame, compared with sucrose, induce greater weight gain in adult Wistar rats, at similar caloric intake levels. Appetite 2013 Jan;60(1):203-7.

Ferzak, Franz.:Nikola Tesla. Michaels-Vertrieb, Peiting 1995

Flanagan, Patrick, Gael Crystal: Elixier der Jugendlichkeit. Du bist, was Du trinkst. 1998

Gassen Hans Günter, Minol, Sabine: Unbekanntes Wesen Gehirn, Media Team 2004

Hacheney, Wilfried: Organische Physik. Wasser-Mensch-Kräfte, Peiting 2001

Honauer, Urs: Wasser. Die geheimnisvolle Energie. Hugendubel, München 1998

Howarth, M. et al.: Association of water softness and heavy alcohol consumption with higher hospital admission rates for alcoholic liver disease. Alcohol & Alcoholism. Nov/Dec2012, 47(6):688-696

Jebens, Klaus. Die Urkraft aus dem Universum, Jupiter Verlag, Zürich 2013

Kaiser-Alexnat, Renate: Wonder Woad. Experiences involving human and plant. epubli 2013.

Kelder, Peter: Die Fünf »Tibeter«®: Das alte Geheimnis aus den Hochtälern des Himalaja. Bern 1999

Klinghardt, Dietrich: Schwermetalle – Vergiftung und Entgiftung, Vortrag im Rahmen eines Seminars über Psycho-Kinesiologie, auf Schloss Elmau bei Garmisch-Partenkirchen, 20 Nov. 1996

Kroeger, Hanna: Arteriosclerosis and Herbal Chelation, H. Kroeger Publ. 84

Kushi, Michio: Die makrobiotische Antwort auf Krebs: Die Ernährungs- und Lebensweise entscheidet über Verhütung und Überwindung von Krebs, Mahajiva Verlag, 1989Lai, H, Singh, N.P.: Acute low-intensity microwave exposure increases DNA single-strand breaks in rat brain cells. Bioelectrom. 1995 16(3): 207-10

Leong, C.C. et al.: Retrograde degeneration of neurite membrane structural integrity of nerve growth cones following in vitro exposure to mercury. Neuroreport 12 (2001) 733-37

Liao,YH et al.: Magnesium in drinking water modifies the association between nitrate ingestion and risk of death from esophageal cancer. J Toxicol Environ Health A 2013;76(3):192-200

Meyer, M. E.: Selbsthilfe-Heilbuch, Aitrang 2005 So halt ich mir den Arzt vom Leib, Aachen 2011

Moritz, Andreas: Timeless Secrets of Health and Rejuvenation, 5th edition, 2009

Mutter, J. et al.: Does inorganic mercury play a role in Alzheimer's disease? A systematic review and an integrated molecular mechanism, J Alzheimers Dis. 2010;22(2):357-74. doi: 10.3233/JAD-2010-100705.

Neumann, Halima: Stop der Azidose, Allergien und Haarausfall, Starnberg 1994

Olney JW et al.: Increasing brain tumor rates: is there a link to aspartame? J Neuropathol Exp Neurol. 1996 Nov;55(11):1115-23.

Ott, Rainer J. : Wassertest. Löwensteinstr. 4A, 97828 Marktheidenfeld, OT Michelrieth. Tel. 09394-994500, Fax 10

Ouhtit A et al.: Chemoprevention of rat mammary carcinogenesis by Spirulina, Am J Pathol.2013

Rosen von, Jürgen: Die Dr. von Rosen-Kur: Entschlackung, Ernährung, Bewegung, ganz natürlich gesund, Egg/ZH 2008

Schauberger, Viktor. Unsere sinnlose Arbeit - die Ursache des biologischen Bankrotts. Impl 11/12, 1963

Schernhammer, Eva. S. et al: Consumption of artificial sweetener- and sugar-containing soda and risk of lymphoma and leukemia in men and woman Am, J Clin Nutr. 2013 Aug;98(2):512

Schwenk, Theodor: Das sensible Chaos. Stuttgart 1962

Sheldrake, Rupert: Das schöpferische Universum. Berlin 1993

Silva, José: The Silva Mind Control Method, NY 1991

Simonsohn, Barbara: Warum Bio? Gesunde Pflanze, gesunder Mensch, München 2002

Takashi K. et al: Regression analysis of cancer incidence rates and water fluoride in the U.S.A. based on IACR/IARC (WHO) data (1978-1992) International Agency for Research on Cancer.J Epidemol. 2001 Jul;11(4):170-9

Tesla, Nikola: Wegbereiter der neuen Medizin, Vorträge, Artikel und Erfindungen. ISBN 3- 89539-244-8, Band VI. Michaels Verlag, Peiting Tesla World, Spreitenbach, Schweiz Seine Werke 1997, Edition Nikola Tesla, ISBN 3-89539-247-2

Thomas, Karen: Media Relations, Univ. of Calgary www.talkinternational.com/nralzheimers.htm

Trincher, Karl S. In: Urs Honauer, Wasser, die geheinisvolle Energie, S. 141 f.

Turtur, Claus W.: Die Angst vieler Physiker vor der Raumenergie. In: Energierevolution, 2.2.2013

Vörösmarety, CJ, McIntyre, PB et al. Global threats to human water security and river bio-diversity. Nature. 2010 Nov 11;468(7321):334 3.,

Volkamer, Klaus: Die feinstoffliche Erweiterung unseres Weltbildes: Ansatz einer erweiterten Physik zur unbegrenzten Gewinnung Freier Energie aus der Feinstofflichkeit, Berlin 2013

Wagner, M., Oehlmann, J.: Endocrine disruptors in bottled mineral water: total estrogenic burden and migration from plastic bottles. In: Environmental Science and Pollution Research, Vol 16, Issue 3, 2009. S. 278–286

Wagner, M., Oehlmann, J.: Endocrine disruptors in bottled mineral water: Estrogenic activity in the E-Screen. In: The Journal of Steroid Biochemistry and Mol Bio, Vol 127, 1–2, 2011. S.128-135

Walton, Ralph: Seizure and Mania After High Intake of Aspartame. Psychosom.1986 27:218-20

Winneke, G. Et al.: Behavioral Sexual Dimorphism in School-Age Children and Early Developmental Exposure to Dioxins and PCBs: A Follow-Up Study of the Duisburg Cohort. Environ Health Perspect. 2013 Nov 22

Index

The illustrated trip to Morocco is a very personal one, amusingly told and highly motivating. Not only in terms of traveling in a motorhome, also in respect of the healthy and spiritual life. The PhD nutritionist lets her readers know how to stay happy, well, slim and beautiful up to old age. Previous readers of this exciting experience report announce to have had the feeling of being always close to the action. They could not stop reading. Literary tidbits are the descriptions of the Neckar valley, the historical review and the snow storm & robbery in France. The snowy Atlas Peak, the hustle and bustle at Square Djemaa el-Fna, the dangerous carriage ride in Marrakesh and the water traps at Ouzoud waterfall are other highlights.

If one expects detailed data on places and attractions will be disappointed. The author has learned that the travelers in apartment on wheels should better not rely on info in travel guides. For what is still a pitch-tip today may already be locked with 2 m high beams. Yet, the book contains lots of tips for globetrotters who want to outsmart the winter in the stunningly beautiful country with its cheerful and affectionate residents.

ISBN 978-3738609578 94 pages € 7,90

Marianne Meyer is via her mother related to Doris Day. She wanted to have a personal present for her 90th birthday. Thus, she wrote and illustrated this autobiographical novel. That way Doris gets an idea of how her darling grandmother's life would have been, if she'd not have emigrated to Massachusetts. Some of her Neckar relatives posed on the ferry for Doris. The author also has high hopes that her famous relative has connections in the Carmel area. She also wants to find her father's grandfather's folks. M. Meyer learned about this family mystery on a higher level of consciousness, which a few months later, her mother revealed to her strolling through the very place, he had supposed to have settled - in Carmel.

The author's secondary subjects have to do with past lives, other spheres of perception, synchronicities, and prophetic dreams. On her mother's side, the second face is a common phenomenon. The more tangible fields, in which she allowed herself to train at three academies could not dissuade her from the cosmic laws. She knows from experience that besides the visible world are other worlds, independent of space and time.

ISBN 978-3735792822 190 pages €12,90

With her bestseller *Spirulina, das blaugrüne Wunder* and an appearance on ARD Prime TV, the author made the microalgae known in the German-speaking area. Since then, more and more people supplement their diets with the protein-rich *Green Gold*. Also, more and more dentists use Spirulina for discharging amalgam and other toxins.

Sensational studies and reports around the globe prove: We can strengthen our immune with Spirulina and stand up to pain, depression, diabetes, MS, cataracts, allergies, anemia, arthritis, liver fibrosis, Parkinson's, and even AIDS, cancer and radioactive radiation. We need the *nerve nourishment* now more than ever. Because it strengthens the heart, makes you fit and slim, provides for healthy eyes, skin and hair, deacidification and regenerates all organs. Particularly benefit the sick, convalescent, heavy laborers, athletes, stressed mothers, hyperactive children, the elderly and busy managers of Spirulina. In the illustrated book with delicious new recipes, the hurried reader can acquire a compact knowledge of the natural food supplement no. 1 in 30 minutes via collected random chapter summaries. It will be soon available in English.

100 pages   € 7,99

The body's own defenses are true miracles of the creation: they surround us with a natural shield. The self-help remedies book shows how we can give our immune system what it needs to protect us from harm. This inner healer can serve us like a finely tuned instrument, on conditions that we follow the *Seven Rules for a long and healthy life.* These include detoxification, exercises, diet secrets, and cleansing treatments.

Whether we enjoy the zest of life depends on these few essential health regulations. With Marianne E. Meyer, you have a versatile expert with a great pioneering spirit on your side. She inspires you to live your best by giving the best of you: your talents. If, e. g., you love to sing, make your hobby your profession. Or join a choir as the author united with the *East Algarve International Shanty Choir.* Singing strengthens evidently the immune system. In the book, you'll find guidance to achieve your objectives.

This new illustrated easy to read edition, comes with collected random chapter summaries, and the essentials are written in bold letters. It will be available in fall 2015.

100 pages   €7,99